To my darling – may we fea
style for eve

Christmas '09

with love, N

CAPE TOWN FOOD

The way we eat in Cape Town today.

CAPE TOWN FOOD

PHILLIPPA CHEIFITZ

**PHOTOGRAPHY
JAC DE VILLIERS**

Struik Publishers
(a division of New Holland Publishing
   (South Africa) (Pty) Ltd)
Cornelis Struik House
80 McKenzie Street
Cape Town 8001
South Africa

www.struik.co.za

New Holland Publishing is a member of
   Avusa Ltd

First published in 2002
10 9 8 7 6 5 4

Publishing manager: Linda de Villiers
Editor: Cecilia Barfield
Designer: Petal Palmer
Design assistant: Sean Robertson
Photographer: Jac de Villiers
Food stylist: Phillippa Cheifitz
Food preparation: Andrea Steer
Proofreader and indexer: Joy Clack
Repro consultant: Farouk Abrahams

Reproduction by Hirt & Carter Cape (Pty) Ltd
Printed and bound by Sing Cheong Printing
   Company Limited

ISBN 978 1 86872 716 2

Log on to our photographic website
www.imagesofafrica.co.za
for an African experience.

Cover photograph shot on location shot at Den Anker
restaurant, Pierhead, V&A Waterfront.
Photograph on page 1 shot on location at Cape Town
Tourism, The Clocktower Precint, V&A Waterfront.

CONTENTS

In memory of my mother Rose and my sister Eileen.
And for Robert, Jann, Stephen, Tony and Gabriel.
With love.

There are many beautiful places in the world, but having travelled east and west and lived north, I believe that there is no other city as exquisite as Cape Town. It has mountains that touch the sea and a sun that sets over the ocean. A true Capetonian, who leaves the city for a time, yearns to return. To see Table Mountain. To climb it once again. To walk along the ocean.

The climate, typical of islands and peninsulas, is changeable and sometimes windy – often very windy. The Southeaster, the strong summer wind, is also more endearingly known as the Cape Doctor for it blows the air clean. But most days are perfect, sunny and warm, not humid. It's a feel-good climate. Cape Town is greenest in winter when the rain falls, which it doesn't all the time, and sometimes it's hard to tell winter from summer.

Our food too, the way we cook today, is casual, using excellent local ingredients. It's gutsy, earthy food, full of flavour. Settlers, each in turn, have made their mark. The Portuguese thought of staying, but sadly the wind that day turned them away. Today Portuguese, mainly from Angola and Mozambique, make up one of the larger communities outside Portugal. The more stoic Dutch, master gardeners at home, arrived in 1652, determined to provide fresh produce to the ships that stopped on the way to and from the lucrative spice islands of the East. From Indonesia they also brought slaves, many of them educated political prisoners. The women made good cooks, the men expert fishermen. The French Huguenots came to escape persecution at home. The British wrenched the colony from the Dutch at the end of the 18th century. In the 1950s, the Italians introduced cappuccino and lasagne in casual coffee bars to a society that was more familiar with the formality of hotel grill rooms and department store tea rooms. Today, an invasion of restaurateurs, from Brussels to Bangkok, have expanded our range of eating experiences to encompass the globe.

We have a long history of hospitality in the Cape. Lady Anne Barnard, wife of the Colonial Secretary during the first British Occupation, wrote of the elegant entertaining in the splendid reception halls of the Castle, Groot Constantia and Vergelegen. And now that Cape Town, blissfully, is an open, democratic city, we welcome the many visitors that come to marvel at one of the world's wonders.

REFERENCE
The South African Culinary Tradition by Renata Coetzee (Struik Publishers)

INTRODUCTION

CATCH OF THE DAY

The thing about fish is that it has to be fresh. Your dish is as good as your fish so quality is more important than culinary expertise. Precision-timing keeps fish moist and delicious. Flash it in the pan, sear it under the grill or slap it on the barbecue. All fish needs is some good quality olive oil, smashed garlic, crushed fresh herbs and the essential squeeze of lemon. So cherish a trustworthy fishmonger. Better a small selection, and a fresh choice each day. Nothing beats fish straight off the boat, and a visit to Kalk Bay harbour, around noon, promises an unforgettable excursion plus an exemplary dinner.

catch of the day

seared salmon trout salad

herbed calamari salad

cape fish soup with lemon

mayo and garlic crostini

grilled marinated fish

roast centre-cut fish

with vegetables

roast fish with

garlic-herb dressing

baked fish and fennel

with lemon vinaigrette

new-style fish and chips

fish and vegetable

parcels

lemon cream risotto

with crayfish

pasta with seafood and

mushroom sauce

roasted prawns with chilli oil

and coriander

PAGES 8/9 Kalk Bay harbour.

LEFT Smoked snoek is a Cape delicacy, best enjoyed like smoked salmon, with a squeeze of lemon juice and a twist of black pepper. Or serve it with a tomato sambal, a Cape Malay favourite – chopped red tomatoes, onion, chilli and a douse of vinegar, seasoned to taste. I add lots of chopped fresh coriander leaves, and sometimes a spoon of olive oil.

seared salmon trout salad

500 g small potatoes, scrubbed and halved
4 fresh salmon trout fillets, with skin
olive oil

for the dressing
3 Tbsp white wine vinegar
⅓ cup olive oil
milled Atlantic sea salt and black pepper
3 or 4 salad onions, chopped
2–3 Tbsp chopped Italian parsley

for serving
salad leaves for 4 – any mix of chicory, curly
endive, radicchio or rocket

First boil the potatoes until tender.

To make the dressing, first whisk the vinegar
with the oil and seasoning to taste. Add the
onions and parsley. Mix half the dressing with
the hot potatoes.

To cook the trout, moisten the skin side of
each fillet with olive oil. Place the salmon
skin-side down in a cold non-stick pan. Turn
the heat to high and leave until the skin is
crisp. Don't flip – the flesh will be just cooked,
still moist and a beautiful colour.

Place a pile of salad leaves on each plate.
Add potatoes and top with a seared trout
fillet. Spoon over the rest of the dressing.

for 4

Pretty good salmon trout is
farmed in Franschhoek. It comes
fresh, smoked (hot and cold)
or cured Swedish-style as
gravadlax. You could of course
use hot-smoked salmon trout
fillets for the salad instead.

herbed calamari salad

500 g cleaned calamari, sliced

for the dressing
1 cup shredded basil leaves
¼ cup finely chopped parsley
¼ cup chopped coriander leaves
4 spring onions, thinly sliced
⅔ cup fresh lemon juice
1 cup olive oil
2 fat cloves garlic, crushed
1 tsp salt
milled black pepper to taste

for serving
2 sticks celery, thinly sliced or
1 bulb fennel, thinly sliced
shredded crisp lettuce or soft lettuce leaves

First mix together all the ingredients for the dressing. Set aside.

Drop the calamari slices into a saucepan of boiling salted water. Cook for barely a minute until just opaque (it's overcooking that toughens calamari).

Drain well and mix with the dressing. Marinate overnight in the refrigerator.

Add celery or fennel and mix together. Turn onto a platter or onto individual plates and garnish with lettuce.

for 4

cape fish soup with lemon mayo and garlic crostini

1 red stumpnose (1.5–2 kg)
1 onion, sliced
2–3 Tbsp olive oil
1 bulb fennel or 2–3 leeks, sliced
1 head garlic, halved
strips of lemon and orange peel, soaked in boiling water
1 ripe red whole tomato
1 bay leaf
a few sprigs of celery and parsley sprigs
fennel fronds (optional)
½ cup dry white wine
8 cups water
a few peppercorns
1 tsp salt
chopped parsley to garnish

for the lemon mayonnaise
1 extra-large free-range egg or
2 free-range egg yolks, at room temperature
milled Atlantic sea salt and black pepper
2 Tbsp strained lemon juice
1–2 cups sunflower oil
2–3 Tbsp olive oil
1 Tbsp boiling water

garlic crostini (see page 32)

Ask your fishmonger to skin and fillet the fish, but take home the head and bones.

Gently soften the onion in olive oil. Add the fennel or leeks, garlic, citrus peel, tomato, bay leaf, celery, parsley, fennel fronds, fish head and bones, wine, water, peppercorns and salt. Slowly bring to the boil, then simmer, half-covered, for about half an hour.

Strain and check seasoning. If necessary, reduce over a high heat to intensify the flavour. Strain the broth again through a colander lined with a new disposable cloth.

Cut the fish into six pieces and, just before serving, poach in the hot broth for about 5 minutes until opaque and just cooked.

For the mayonnaise, blend or process the egg or yolks with seasoning and lemon juice. Gradually add enough sunflower oil to make a thick mayonnaise, add some olive oil, and finally, boiling water to make it shiny.

Place a piece of fish in a wide bowl. Top with one or two garlic-rubbed crostini and a dollop of mayonnaise. Ladle over the broth and sprinkle with chopped parsley.

for 6

grilled marinated fish

1 kg filletted fresh line fish, in 1 or 2 pieces
coarse salt
3 Tbsp melted butter
paprika

for the marinade
juice of 1 large lemon
3 Tbsp dry white wine
3 Tbsp olive oil
1 tsp soy sauce
1 clove garlic, crushed
1 Tbsp chopped fresh dill
milled black pepper

Rinse the fish. Sprinkle with salt and leave in the refrigerator for an hour or two to firm. Wash off the salt and pat dry. Make a few diagonal slashes and place on an oiled ovenproof pan.

Mix together all the ingredients for the marinade. Pour over the fish and leave to marinate for at least 30 minutes.

Add the melted butter and a sprinkling of paprika. Slide under a hot grill and cook for 8–10 minutes, or until a good colour, opaque, just firm to the touch but still moist. Serve immediately with steamed potatoes and stir-fried green vegetable or side salad.

for 4

Local favourites
Cape salmon, yellowtail and kabeljou are well-loved line fish. Red and white stumpnose and steenbras are prized. Silver steenbras is another name for the excellent musselcracker, sometimes available. Hake is plentiful and used in the national fast food dish of fried fish and chips – never say the British didn't have a strong culinary influence. Kingklip is considered a delicacy by many, and cooked with care, results in the texture that earned its reputation. Pan-fried, lightly-battered soles are also a great favourite. Angel-fish is a good value substitute. And freshly caught snoek in season, best from cold waters, is integral to the Cape, whether fried, barbecued or, particularly, smoked.

roast centre-cut fish with vegetables

8 medium potatoes, peeled and
thickly sliced
8 carrots, peeled and thickly sliced
3–4 onions, quartered
1 or 2 whole heads garlic, unpeeled
olive oil
milled Atlantic sea salt and black pepper
2 kg centre-cut piece of fish
(red steenbras, Cape salmon or yellowtail)
juice of 1 lemon
2 fat cloves garlic, crushed
a few sprigs of rosemary

Arrange the potatoes, carrots, onions and
heads of garlic in a roasting pan. Moisten with
olive oil and season. Roast at 190 °C for
20 minutes. Make space for the fish in the
centre and add it to the pan.

Score the fish lightly, mix together ½ cup of
olive oil, lemon juice and crushed garlic, and
pour over the fish.

Tuck in sprigs of rosemary. Roast at 190 °C for
45 minutes, turning the vegetables now and
again until the fish feels firm when pressed and
the vegetables are tender.

Squeeze the roasted garlic cloves over the
portions of fish and vegetables.

for 6

Your choice, as always, will depend on what's freshest.
I'm fond of cooking fish this way, as the two large fillets are easy
to fit in the oven and to dish up at the table.
But don't forget to take home the head and bones to make
the delicious spiced rice featured on page 85.
I do believe that dousing the hot fish with the marinade as
it comes out the oven has a stronger impact than cooking it in the
marinade. Serve the fish straight from the oven or at room
temperature. Any leftovers make a good salad.

roast fish with garlic-herb dressing

1.5–2 kg whole fish (Cape salmon, kabeljou or
yellowtail), filletted
milled Atlantic sea salt and black pepper
olive oil

for the dressing
juice of 1 large lemon
2–3 fat cloves garlic, crushed
⅔ cup olive oil
a generous handful of coriander or
basil leaves, chopped
milled Atlantic sea salt and black pepper

Wash the fish and salt it, then refrigerate to firm until ready to cook.

Rinse off the salt and dry very well. Grind over some pepper and moisten with olive oil. Arrange the two large fillets of fish in an oiled roasting pan and roast, one rack above the middle, at 240 °C for 10 minutes, or until just cooked and still moist.

Mix together the dressing and spoon it over the fish as soon as it comes out of the oven. If I've used coriander in the dressing, I serve the dish with the spiced rice. I may make an avocado sauce, mashing one or two avocados with lemon juice, chopped chilli, coriander leaves and, of course, seasoning to taste.

With basil, I put out a bowl of thick home-made mayonnaise and baked or steamed potatoes, in which case I freeze the head and bones to use later.

for 4–6

Freshly caught and quickly cleaned
For a few rands, have your fresh fish cleaned
at Kalk Bay harbour.

baked fish and fennel with lemon vinaigrette

8 bulbs baby fennel, split in half
sunflower oil for searing
½ cup fish or vegetable stock
1–2 Tbsp olive oil
4 portions filletted fish, with skin
4 pats butter

for the lemon vinaigrette
juice of 1 large lemon
⅓ cup olive oil
milled Atlantic sea salt and black pepper

for serving
a side dish of steamed new baby potatoes

First, sear the fennel on top of the stove in hot sunflower oil, then cook in the oven, with stock and a spoonful or two of olive oil, at 180 °C for about 20 minutes, or until tender-crisp.

Wash the fish and pat dry. Sear, skin-side down only, on top of the stove in hot sunflower oil, until crisp. Top each fillet with a pat of butter and complete cooking in the oven at 180 °C for 5–10 minutes, or until just cooked. Remove the fennel, with a slotted spoon, to plates or a platter. Place the fish on top

Whisk together all the ingredients for the vinaigrette and spoon it over the fish. Turn over the fish to present it skin-side up.

for 4

Fishcakes
A Cape favourite, fishcakes are sold at every fish and chip shop. Use a can of lowly pilchards or the luxury of salmon trout, both equally rich in omega-3 oil. Mix together 1 can flaked pilchards or 400–500 g flaked, steamed fish with 400–500 g mashed potatoes, 1 fried chopped onion, 2–3 Tbsp chopped parsley or dill, 2–3 Tbsp thick homemade mayonnaise, a good squeeze of lemon juice and seasoning to taste. Chill to firm or thicken with fresh breadcrumbs. Shape into flattish cakes and dip in flour, then in beaten free-range egg. Shallow-fry in hot oil, until well-browned on both sides. for 4-6

new-style fish and chips

for each serving

1 x 200 g portion fresh fish, filletted

milled Atlantic sea salt and black pepper

large baking potatoes, cut into
thick wedges

olive oil

1 wedge lemon or ½ lime

Lightly salt the fish and set aside.

Moisten the potatoes lightly with olive oil and arrange in a single layer in an oiled roasting pan. Roast, one rack above the middle, at 250 °C for 20 minutes. Turn and roast for another 10 minutes, or until golden brown and tender.

Meanwhile wash and dry the fish. Moisten with olive oil and season with pepper. Sear on top of the stove over high heat, then place in the hot oven for a few minutes until barely cooked and still moist.

Serve with lemon wedges or lime halves. Another option is to pass around basil or coriander pesto.

for 1

Mussels at Den Anker
with a view of Table Mountain

Our local West Coast mussels, farmed at Saldanha, are popular served Belgian-style, at local Belgian eateries. The mussels are flavoured with onion and celery, then steamed in dry white wine, just until they open.

Serve with *pommes frites*, homemade mayonnaise for dipping, and crusty baguette for dunking in the mussel broth.

fish and vegetable parcels

for each serving

a thick square of filletted fish

slim vegetable strips (any mix of carrot, baby
marrow, celery or spring onion, or whatever's
in season) or whole baby spring green
vegetables (mangetout or snow peas, fine
green beans and asparagus tips)

for the sauce

2 Tbsp soft or melted butter

1 tsp fresh lemon juice

1 small clove garlic, crushed

½ tsp soy sauce

a few sprigs thyme or chopped
parsley (or both)

milled Atlantic sea salt and black pepper

Pat the fish quite dry and place in the centre of a large piece of well-oiled greaseproof paper. Strew generously with the vegetables.

Mix all the sauce ingredients together and pour over the fish. Wrap up well, twisting the top securely. If you oil the paper on the outside, it will have a nice sheen.

Bake at 230 °C for 10 minutes, or until the fish is just cooked and the vegetables are tender-crisp.

Serve the parcels in their wrapping on large plates. Provide a side dish of mash or steamed potato slices to mop up juices.

for 1

lemon cream risotto with crayfish

3 Tbsp unsalted butter
3 Tbsp olive oil
1 punnet baby fennel or leeks, thinly sliced
1 onion, finely chopped
zest of 1 large bright lemon, finely shredded
2 cups Italian risotto rice
6–8 cups hot home-made chicken
or fish broth
½ cup fresh cream, heated
1–2 Tbsp strained lemon juice
milled Atlantic sea salt and black pepper
4 fresh crayfish tails
olive oil or melted butter for searing

for serving
fennel fronds or Italian parsley

Heat the butter and oil in a wide pan. Add the fennel or leeks and onion, and cook very gently until soft but still pale.

Meanwhile, pour boiling water over shreds of lemon zest and drain after a few minutes.

Stir the rice into the softened vegetable mixture until well coated. Add the zest. Adding a ladleful of broth at a time, cook over a brisk heat, stirring constantly to prevent catching, for 25 minutes.

Once the rice is swollen and moist, stir in the cream. Allow to heat through. Add lemon juice and seasoning to taste.

Meanwhile, brush the crayfish tails with olive oil or melted butter. Sear in a hot pan on top of the stove or under a fierce grill until just cooked and moist and starting to catch. Or if you prefer, steam the tails in wine and water with a handful of herbs.

Serve the risotto in wide bowls topped with a crayfish tail and garnished with fennel fronds or Italian parsley.

for 4

On track
Local train passing through Kalk Bay.

pasta with seafood and mushroom sauce

500 g spaghettini or linguine, cooked
and drained

for the sauce
1½ cups fish stock
½ cup dry white wine
a few sprigs of parsley, dill and celery
250 g peeled prawns, defrosted,
rinsed and dried
250 g baby calamari tubes, thinly sliced
500 g cleaned, tightly closed mussels
250 g mushrooms, thinly sliced
1 cup fresh cream
2 cloves garlic, crushed
3 Tbsp chopped dill
milled Atlantic sea salt and black pepper
chopped dill for sprinkling

For the sauce, bring the stock, wine and sprigs of herbs to a bubble. Add the prawns and simmer for a minute at most. Remove with a large slotted spoon.

Add the calamari and simmer for barely a minute, until opaque. Remember it's overcooking that toughens calamari. Remove with a large slotted spoon.

Add the mussels (discarding any that aren't tightly closed) and simmer for a few minutes until they open. Remove with a slotted spoon. Discard those that haven't opened.

Fish out the herbs and discard.

Add the mushrooms, cream, garlic and dill and simmer briskly until reduced and slightly thickened. Return the seafood to the sauce and heat through. Season to taste. Toss with hot pasta and sprinkle with dill.

for 4–6

roasted prawns with chilli oil and coriander

500 g large Mozambique
prawns, deveined
½ cup olive oil
2 fresh red chillies, chopped
3 Tbsp chopped coriander
3 cloves garlic, crushed
milled Atlantic sea salt and black pepper
lemon wedges for serving

Heat the oven to a fierce 240 °C.

Rinse the prawns and pat dry.

Heat the oil with the chillies in a roasting pan large enough to take the prawns in a single layer. Add the prawns to the hot oil and roast for 5 minutes. Remove from the oven and add the coriander and garlic. Turn the prawns around to coat. Roast for another 5 minutes or until the prawns are pink and curled. Add seasoning to taste.

Serve with lemon wedges. Put out a bowl of rice steamed with baby spinach leaves, and a good mixed salad dressed with olive oil and lemon juice on the side.

for 3–4

Cape Town began as a garden. The successful Dutch East India Company, importing spices from Asia, needed a halfway house to replenish supplies for ships as they rounded the Cape. Jan van Riebeeck was sent to oversee this difficult task. He persevered and, within six months of his arrival in April 1652, served a dinner that more than impressed his guests, officers from the ship *Goede Hoop*. Fresh asparagus, peas and spinach accompanied the main course. By 1685 Francois Valentyn, a visitor to the Cape, described the Cape as comparable in beauty to the legendary Hanging Gardens of Babylon. The Company Gardens are still a focal point of Cape Town, at the top of Adderley Street, next to the Avenue behind the Houses of Parliament. The café is a good outdoor stop when visiting local museums – the Natural History Museum, the National Art Gallery

the   market   place

and the Jewish Museum. An old-fashioned menu boasts Cape Town favourites, a pot of tea with anchovy toast, apple pie and cream, fried fish and chips and, in summer, half a sweet melon with a scoop of vanilla ice cream. Today the Gardens are botanical. We buy fresh produce from greengrocers, supermarkets, open markets, from the back of a lorry or from street hawkers.

PAGES 28/29 Eeltje Botsma of The Olive Branch Nursery sells farm-fresh produce, Tuesdays and Fridays, outside one of Cape Town's most popular food shops, Giovanni's Deliworld, where locals meet for espresso and cappuccino.

ABOVE Cape Town chef Gawie le Roux picks herbs in the garden at The Castle of Good Hope that dates back to 1666.

herbed avocado and

ricotta spread

pasta with onion sauce

and stir-fried greens

roasted winter vegetables

sheet sweet potatoes

smashed baked potatoes

baked cabbage and

cheese casserole

chicken with

waterblommetjies and

egg and lemon sauce on

baked risotto

chilled red soup

fresh green

asparagus frittata

carrots with naartjie

and coriander

roasted beetroot with

citrus dressing

herbed avocado and ricotta spread

1 large ripe avocado, skinned and cubed
250 g ricotta cheese
½ cup chopped fresh herbs
(basil, parsley or coriander, or a mix)
1–2 Tbsp fresh lemon juice
(or more to taste)
2 Tbsp olive oil
salt and milled black pepper to taste

Blend all the ingredients together. Turn into a bowl and cover with a piece of clingfilm placed directly on the surface. Allow to firm up in the refrigerator.

for 6

Good with crusty baguette or crisp crostini. Great as a dip too, with crunchy sticks of cucumber and celery, carrot and sweet pepper, or small whole Cos lettuce leaves or chicory.

To make crostini, oven-toast slices of panini or baguette at 190 °C for 10–15 minutes, or until pale golden and crisp. If desired, rub with a half-head of garlic.

pasta with onion sauce and stir-fried greens

300 g thin fresh pasta

for the sauce
2 large onions, finely chopped
salt and milled black pepper
2 Tbsp unsalted butter
2 Tbsp olive oil
1 clove garlic, crushed
2 Tbsp chopped sage leaves
1 cup chicken or vegetable stock
½ cup fresh cream

for the greens
50 g baby spinach leaves (or tatsoi)
50 g rocket leaves
50 g watercress
2 Tbsp olive oil
1 tsp balsamic vinegar

for serving
shavings of parmesan cheese
fresh chives, snipped

To make the sauce, gently cook the onions with a pinch of salt, covered, in the heated butter and oil for about 30 minutes or until meltingly soft. If necessary, add a little water to prevent catching.

Stir in the garlic, sage and a little seasoning. Pour in the stock and cream and simmer for about 5 minutes, or until slightly reduced.

Mix with pasta that has just been cooked and drained, then check seasoning.

Meanwhile, stir-fry the washed and dried greens in the heated oil until wilted. Add the balsamic vinegar. Spoon over the pasta and sauce. Top with shavings of parmesan and garnish with chives.

for 4

**The creamy onions
are also good spread
on crostini stuck with bits
of anchovy or olive.**

roasted winter vegetables

1 bunch carrots
1 bunch parsnips
1 bunch turnips
1 bunch swedes or a wedge of pumpkin
1 bunch leeks
salt and milled black pepper
olive oil
a few sprigs rosemary and thyme

Peel and cut the vegetables into chunks, or leave small vegetables whole. Arrange in a single layer in an oiled roasting pan. Season, moisten with oil and tuck in sprigs of herbs.

Roast at 230 °C, one shelf above the middle of the oven, for about 40 minutes, or until tender and beginning to catch.

Serve with roasted lamb or fish. Or serve as a vegetarian dish with brown rice or soft polenta and parmesan.

to roast with chicken

Butterfly a free-range chicken and place it on top of the vegetables. Season and oil the chicken and roast at 230 °C for 45 minutes to 1 hour, or until brown and crisp and the vegetables are tender.

to serve as a salad

Turn the roasted vegetables onto a platter and tuck in radicchio and chicory leaves, or lots of rocket. Add a little more seasoning and moisten with good olive oil and a judicious amount of balsamic vinegar.

to turn into a soup

10 cups water
1 cup barley
½ cup parsley sprigs
3–4 sticks celery, roughly cut
1–2 onions, halved
1 Tbsp salt
1 bay leaf
a few peppercorns
salt and milled black pepper
chopped parsley for sprinkling

Simmer the water with the barley, parsley, celery, onions, salt, bay leaf and a few peppercorns for about 45 minutes, or until the barley is tender.

Strain the barley (reserving liquid). Discard the bay leaf and peppercorns, then purée the broth with its vegetables and half the roasted vegetables. Add the rest of the roasted vegetables and barley. Check seasoning and heat through. Sprinkle with parsley and serve.

for 6

sheet sweet potatoes

3 medium sweet potatoes (or large regular
baking potatoes)
¼ cup olive oil or 50 g butter, melted
salt and milled black pepper

Scrub the potatoes very well and slice
very thinly, best using a mandoline.

Brush a baking sheet with oil or melted butter.
Arrange the sliced potatoes in overlapping
rows. Season and drizzle over the remaining
oil or butter.

Bake at 260 °C for 15 minutes, or until tender,
golden and crisp. You can lift the whole sheet
to top a casserole, or separate it into
individual portions.

for 6

smashed baked potatoes

for each serving
1 large baking potato
crushed garlic
rosemary leaves
salt and milled black pepper
olive oil

Slit a cross in each potato, then bake at
200 °C for 1 hour, or until tender.

Smash each one with a potato masher
and place in a baking dish. Add garlic
and bits of rosemary to each potato.
Season and moisten with olive oil.

Return to the oven for 5–10 minutes
to heat through.

for 1

baked cabbage and cheese casserole

100–125 g rindless bacon or smoked
sausage, diced
2 cloves garlic, crushed
500–600 g thinly sliced, cored cabbage
5 cups chicken or
vegetable stock
grated nutmeg
salt and milled black pepper
6 slices day-old country-style bread
150 g gruyère cheese, thinly sliced

Stir-fry the bacon or sausage over a high heat until the fat runs. Reduce the heat and add the garlic, then the cabbage. Stirring now and again, cook for about 5 minutes until the cabbage wilts. Add stock, nutmeg to taste and a little seasoning, and simmer for 20–30 minutes.

Toast the bread at 190 °C for about 10 minutes, or until lightly browned.

Place 2 slices of bread on the bottom of an oiled casserole. Remove one-third of the cabbage with a slotted spoon and place over the bread. Top with one-third of the cheese. Repeat with another two layers, then pour over the cabbage liquid to almost cover.

Bake at 190 °C for 45 minutes or until nicely browned and the liquid has almost evaporated.

for 4

Restaurateur's choice
Ondersteun Handelaars at Salt River Market.

PICKED IN MARSHY VLEIS AND DAMS AROUND THE WESTERN CAPE, THESE INDIGENOUS WATER FLOWERS, 'WATERBLOMMETJIES', ARE CONSIDERED A GREAT DELICACY. THE WAXY, FLESHY FLOWER BUDS RANGE IN SHADES FROM GREEN TO SHRIMP TO AMETHYST. ONCE WILD, TODAY THEY ARE FARMED AND EVEN CANNED. TRADITIONALLY SLOWLY COOKED WITH LAMB IN A 'BREDIE', NOW WE USE THEM IN ALL SORTS OF WAYS FROM SOUPS TO QUICHES.

chicken with waterblommetjies and egg and lemon sauce on baked risotto

8 chicken thighs
2 Tbsp sunflower oil
1 onion, thinly sliced
1 clove garlic, crushed
500 g waterblommetjies, well washed
2 Tbsp fresh dill, chopped
1 stick cinnamon
2 cups chicken stock
½ cup dry white wine
fresh dill or wild sorrel flowers to garnish

for the sauce
2 free-range eggs
3 Tbsp fresh lemon juice
salt and milled black pepper

for the baked risotto
2 Tbsp olive oil
1½ cups risotto rice
3 cups hot chicken stock
salt and milled black pepper

Wash and dry the chicken. Brown all over in the heated oil. Remove and set aside.

Reduce the heat and gently soften the onion, adding more oil if required. Stir in the garlic, then return the chicken to the pot.

Add the waterblommetjies, dill and cinnamon and pour in the stock and wine. Bring to a bubble, then reduce heat and simmer for about 40 minutes, or until the chicken and waterblommetjies are very tender. Remove the chicken and waterblommetjies, and keep warm. Leave the cooking liquid in the pot.

To make the sauce, beat the eggs, then gradually beat in the lemon juice and a little of the hot cooking liquid. Gradually whisk into the pot of liquid and cook gently for a few minutes until sightly thickened. Season to taste. Pour over the chicken.

Garnish the chicken with dill and serve with baked risotto.

To make the risotto, heat the olive oil in an ovenproof casserole on top of the stove. Add the rice and stir until coated with oil. Pour in the stock, cover tightly and bake at 180 °C for about 30 minutes, or until the stock is absorbed and the rice is tender and moist. Add seasoning to taste.

for 4–6

chilled red soup

1 kg plum tomatoes
4 large red peppers
olive oil
salt and milled black pepper
1 large red onion, chopped
2 cloves garlic, crushed
3 cups chicken or vegetable stock
thin fresh cream (optional)

for serving
chives and strips of sweet pepper
croutons

Halve the tomatoes lengthways and arrange, cut-side up, in a single layer on a well-oiled baking sheet.

Quarter the peppers and remove the seeds, then arrange them on an oiled baking sheet.

Moisten the vegetables with a little olive oil, add seasoning and roast at 200 °C for about 30 minutes, or until soft.

In a suitable saucepan, gently soften the onion in 2 Tbsp olive oil. Stir in the garlic and roughly chopped roasted vegetables. Add the stock and a little seasoning. Simmer for about 30 minutes.

Purée and check seasoning. Chill well. If you like, add a drizzle of cream.

Garnish with chives and sweet pepper, and serve with croutons.

for 6

fresh green asparagus frittata

500 g slim green asparagus
10 free-range eggs
⅓ cup fresh cream
salt and milled black pepper
2 Tbsp olive oil
grated Italian pecorino cheese

Trim the asparagus and blanch in a large saucepan of boiling, salted water. Drain well.

Beat together the eggs, cream and seasoning to taste.

Heat the olive oil in a large non-stick pan. Pour in the egg mixture and add the asparagus.

Cover (with foil if necessary) and cook over the lowest heat for about 20 minutes or until the eggs are just set and still moist. If you're impatient, slide under a hot grill to quickly set the top.

Sprinkle with cheese and drizzle with olive oil. Cut into wedges for serving. It's good at room temperature.

for 8 as a starter, or 4 as a light meal with a salad

carrots with naartjie and coriander

300 g whole baby carrots
2 naartjies or clementines
1 Tbsp butter
1 tsp honey
1 tsp soy sauce
1 small piece fresh ginger,
peeled and crushed
salt and milled black pepper
fresh coriander leaves to garnish

Scrub the carrots and leave whole.
(If using larger carrots, cut into long, thin strips.)
Place in a heavy or non-stick saucepan with
the rind and juice of the naartjies or
clementines, the butter, honey, soy sauce and
ginger. Cover tightly and cook for 10 minutes
or until tender-crisp. Uncover and reduce the
cooking liquid to a syrupy glaze. Season to
taste and scatter over fresh coriander leaves.

for 4–6

roasted beetroot with citrus dressing

8 medium beetroots
olive oil
sliced red onion and chives to garnish

for the dressing
3 Tbsp fresh orange juice
1 Tbsp fresh lemon juice
½ tsp honey
1 small clove garlic, crushed (optional)
¼ cup olive oil
milled Atlantic sea salt and black
pepper to taste

Scrub the beetroots well. Trim and pat dry.
Line a roasting pan with oiled foil. Lightly oil
the beets. Roast, turning once or twice, at
200 °C for 1 hour or longer, until they can easily
be pierced with a sharp knife. Once the beets
are cool enough, peel and cut them into
segments (wear kitchen gloves).

Mix all the ingredients together for the dressing
and mix with the beetroot. Serve warm, or
cool to room temperature and serve as a
salad garnished with sliced red onion or whole
red spring onions and chives.

for 6

OLIVES AND OIL

black olive spread

roasted vegetable pickle

green minestrone

grilled tuna with haricot bean

salad and gremolata

roasted steak and mushrooms

with pesto and pasta

flat roast chicken with lemons

marinated olives

and anchovies

roasted calamari

seared peppered ostrich

carpaccio

pan-grilled fish

escalopes and pancetta

on greens

o l i v e s   a n d   o i l

Our Cape table olives, both green and black, are known for their high quality. Demand for them is increasing, and exports are growing. Olives ripen from green to purple to black. Olive oil, simply the fresh juice pressed from the fruit, can be extracted at any stage of ripening and can be made from one variety of olive, or a blend from a number of producers.

The first cold-pressing virgin oil is the most esteemed. Heat is needed for a second pressing and this affects the flavour. 'Virgin' refers to the acidity, less than 3% of oleic acids. 'Extra' means that the acidity is less than 1%. Price is not necessarily the key to excellence. Trust your taste, and choose what you like best.

There is an unbelievable variety of olive oils. Italian, French, Spanish, Greek – each has a distinctive character, depending on the type of olive used. Don't neglect our local oils. There's Costa, that goes back to the 1920s, the successful newcomer Morgenster, and the award-winning Vesuvio, one of only three non-Italian oils to receive a quality award at the SOL 2000 exhibition in Verona, and the l'Orciolo d'Oro at the international competition in Pesaro.

When considering which olive oil to use, think of what you're going to do with it. For roasting vegetables or any other kind of cooking, an everyday, good value olive oil from the supermarket is perfectly suitable. The same oil is fine in a dressing or marinade, when mixed with vinegar and other strong flavourings. Keep your finest oil for the table, for annointing a dish or dipping bread.

Store your oil in a cool place, not in the refrigerator where it will go cloudy. But even then, it will clear as it returns to room temperature.

PAGES 46/47 Morgenster Estate, Somerset West.

LEFT Morgenster olive oil for tasting, olive groves, and green olives

black olive spread

1 cup ripe black olives, pitted
50 g anchovy fillets
2 Tbsp capers, rinsed
1 fat clove garlic, crushed
¼ cup olive oil
1 Tbsp fresh lemon juice
milled black pepper

for serving
quarters of crisp red pepper

Pound the olives, anchovies, capers and garlic in a processor. Gradually beat in the oil and lemon juice, and season with black pepper.

Turn into a bowl just large enough to contain it and cover with a film of olive oil.

Use the peppers for dipping or spread onto warmed herb breads (see page 138) or sliced ciabatta.

for 6

Do as the Italians do. At the table, toss salad leaves sparingly with good wine vinegar and season with milled salt and black pepper, then add just enough olive oil to coat the leaves. Generally, proportions are 1 Tbsp vinegar to 4 Tbsp extra-virgin olive oil. If you mix a dressing, you could add a crushed garlic clove or 1 tsp Dijon mustard, or both. If you add chopped fresh herbs, do so just before using, as they lose their freshness when refrigerated.

roasted vegetable pickle

8-10 open brown mushrooms
2-4 cobs corn, thickly sliced
1 small cauliflower, separated into florets
2 large red peppers, seeded
and thickly sliced
500 g butternut or pumpkin chunks
2 onions, cut into wedges
olive oil
a few sprigs rosemary and thyme
8-10 unpeeled garlic cloves
salt and milled black pepper

for the marinade
1 cup white wine vinegar
1½ cups olive oil
3 cloves garlic, crushed
2 bay leaves
a few sprigs parsley, thyme and rosemary
1 Tbsp coriander seeds
2 fresh whole red chillies
1 tsp black peppercorns
1 tsp salt

Arrange the vegetables in 2 large, well-oiled baking trays or shallow roasting pans. Moisten with oil, tuck in sprigs of rosemary and thyme and unpeeled garlic, and season lightly.

Roast at 200 °C or until tender, removing the vegetables as soon as they're done (start checking after 20 minutes). Place the cooked vegetables in a large heatproof glass dish.

Simmer all the marinade ingredients for a few minutes, then pour over the vegetables. Turn over now and again. Store in the refrigerator.

for 8–10

These are great for nibbling. Keep a big jar in the refrigerator.

Serve with crusty bread for dunking in the marinade.

They make terrific sandwiches, on ciabatta bread,

with the addition of thinly sliced mozzarella,

or a pasta salad, tossed with hot pasta and grated parmesan.

green minestrone

Serve hot or cold, depending on the weather. If serving hot, leave out the pasta and ladle the soup over a thick slice of ciabatta.

¼ cup olive oil
1 bunch spring onions, finely chopped
2 leeks, finely chopped
2 sticks celery, finely chopped
1 clove garlic, finely chopped
¼ cup chopped Italian parsley
¼ small cabbage or 2 baby cabbages, finely shredded
250 g baby spinach leaves, well washed and shredded
¾ cup shelled green peas
125 g green beans, thinly sliced
12 green asparagus spears, thinly sliced
125 g baby marrows, diced
salt and milled black pepper
6 cups hot chicken or vegetable stock
½ cup tiny pasta

for serving
shredded basil leaves or
chopped Italian parsley
grated parmesan cheese
good olive oil

In the heated oil, gently cook the spring onions, leeks and celery until starting to soften. Stir in the garlic and parsley and cook for a few minutes.

Add the cabbage and spinach and cook for about 10 minutes. Add the rest of the vegetables and cook for another 5 minutes. Season the vegetables, then pour over the stock. Cover and simmer for 45 minutes.

Stir in the pasta and cook until tender. Check seasoning.

It is more of a stew than a soup, but if you find it too thick, thin down with more stock.

Serve sprinkled with basil or parsley and cheese and a drizzle of olive oil.

for 6

grilled tuna with haricot bean salad and gremolata

for the beans
2 cups haricot beans, soaked overnight
1 bay leaf
a few sprigs rosemary
½ cup olive oil
¼ cup fresh lemon juice
salt and milled black pepper

Drain the beans and place them in a saucepan with fresh water to cover. Add the bay leaf and rosemary but no salt. Simmer, uncovered, for 45 minutes to 1 hour, or until tender. Drain and mix with the olive oil, lemon juice and seasoning to taste. Turn onto a platter.

for the fish
500 g filletted tuna steaks
2 Tbsp olive oil
milled Atlantic sea salt and black pepper

Moisten the fish with olive oil and season. Slide under a hot grill for a few minutes a side until just seared, but still rare and moist. Flake the fish into large pieces and add to the bean salad.

for the gremolata
½ cup finely chopped Italian parsley
2 fat cloves garlic, finely chopped or crushed
4 anchovy fillets, finely chopped
rind of 1 lemon, finely grated and blanched
milled black pepper to taste

To make the gremolata, mix all the ingredients together. Spoon over the gremolata and tuck in rocket leaves. Serve warm or at room temperature.

for 6

for serving
rocket leaves

roasted steak and mushrooms with pesto and pasta

4 thick medallions of beef fillet
olive oil
4 giant open mushrooms
salt and milled black pepper
250 g tagliatelle, cooked and drained
basil for garnishing

for the pesto
2 cups packed fresh basil leaves
2 fat cloves garlic
¼ cup toasted pine nuts
⅔ cup olive oil
½ cup grated parmesan cheese
milled Atlantic sea salt and black pepper

Make the pesto first. Pound the basil and garlic, then mix in the nuts and pound until well blended. Gradually blend in the oil (through the feed tube of a processor) to make a thick paste. Mix in the cheese and seasoning to taste, by hand.

Dry the steaks with paper towel. Remove the mushroom stems, then briefly rinse the caps, or brush well, and pat dry. Moisten with olive oil. Quickly sear the steaks on top of the stove in a heavy pan over a high heat until browned. Remove and season lightly. Do the same with the mushrooms.

Place the steaks and mushrooms in a single layer in a lightly oiled roasting pan and spread thickly with pesto.

Before serving, roast the prepared steaks and mushrooms at 220 °C for 5 minutes, so that the steaks are rare and the mushrooms succulent. Immediately stack the steaks and mushrooms and place on top of hot-drained tagliatelle, first tossed in a little olive oil.

Garnish with basil, pass the parmesan and serve with a side salad of tomatoes.

for 4

flat roast chicken
with lemons and rosemary

1 free-range chicken (about 1.5 kg)
3 bright-skinned lemons
coarse sea salt
3 cloves garlic, crushed
fresh rosemary
milled black pepper
2 Tbsp olive oil
1 cup chicken stock

for olive oil mash
1 kg potatoes, peeled and cut
into 5 cm-thick chunks
6–8 cloves garlic, peeled (optional)
6 Tbsp olive oil
1 cup warm chicken stock
salt and milled black pepper

Split the chicken down the back and open it out as flat as possible. Wash it and dry well.

Pour boiling water over the lemons and leave to stand for 5 minutes. Cut 2 of the lemons in half and rub in coarse salt and crushed garlic. Slice the third lemon thinly, remove any pips and rub in salt.

Arrange the chicken skin-side up in an oiled roasting pan, on a bed of rosemary and the halved, salted lemons. Carefully push the sliced lemons underneath the skin together with bits of rosemary.

Season with milled black pepper. Drizzle the skin with olive oil and roast at 220 °C for 45 minutes, or until crisp and golden. Keep the chicken warm on a heated platter.

Squeeze the pulp from the soft-cooked lemons into the roasting pan and pour in the chicken stock. Taste, if too acidic, add more stock. Reduce slightly over high heat on top of the stove. Check seasoning, then strain before serving.

Serve immediately with olive oil mash (see below) or potatoes roasted in olive oil at the same time as the chicken, and a side salad of mixed greens.

To make the olive oil mash, place the potatoes with the garlic (if using) in a saucepan and cover with cold water. Mix in ½ tsp salt. Bring to the boil, then simmer over a medium heat for 15–20 minutes, or until the potatoes are tender when pierced. Drain well and return to a low heat.

Crush with a potato masher, gradually adding the oil and warm chicken stock. Check seasoning and add salt if necessary, and a grinding of pepper.

for 4–6

marinated olives and anchovies

250 g mixed olives
a few sprigs celery
a few sprigs Italian parsley
1 x 50 g can rolled anchovy fillets
1 red chilli, split
1 clove garlic, crushed
1 Tbsp red wine vinegar
olive oil to cover

Mix the olives with the herbs, anchovies, chilli, garlic and vinegar. Pack into a jar and cover with olive oil. Leave to stand for 1–2 hours, or refrigerate overnight. (Keeps for weeks stored in the refrigerator.) Use leftover marinade as a salad dressing.

for 8 or more

roasted calamari

800 g fresh, small calamari tubes, cleaned
¼ cup olive oil
1 tsp tomato paste
1–2 sprigs rosemary
3 fat cloves garlic, crushed
salt and milled black pepper
chopped parsley for sprinkling
lemon wedges for serving

Pat the calamari dry. Mix the olive oil with the tomato paste, rosemary, garlic and some seasoning. Toss with the well-dried calamari and spread the calamari out in a single layer on a roasting pan. Roast at 250 °C for 10 minutes, or until just done, tender and starting to catch. Sprinkle with parsley and serve with lemon wedges. Good with roasted potato wedges (see page 21) or French fries and a green salad on the side.

for 4

seared peppered ostrich carpaccio

4 portions (500 g) ostrich fillet
coarsely cracked black pepper
best olive oil
30 g rocket leaves
shavings of Parmesan
sea salt flakes

Pat the meat dry, then coat with coarsely cracked pepper and moisten with oil. Sear in a hot, non-stick pan until browned outside, but still rare inside. Leave to rest, then slice thinly and arrange on 4–6 plates. Add rocket leaves and shavings of Parmesan. Drizzle with oil and season with salt.

for 4–6

pan-grilled fish escalopes and pancetta on greens

8 escalopes filleted fish
olive oil
8 slices pancetta

for the marinade
¼ cup balsamic vinegar
2 cloves garlic, crushed
¼ cup olive oil
salt and milled black pepper to taste

for serving
baby greens for 4
4 limes, halved

Pat the fish dry. Mix the marinade ingredients together and mix with the fish.

Heat a ridged, cast-iron pan brushed with oil. Pan-grill the fish for barely 1 minute a side, until just cooked through and still moist. Pan-grill the pancetta until it starts to crisp. Sandwich the fish with the pancetta and stack on portions of baby greens. Heat any remaining marinade and, together with the pan juices, pour over the salad. Serve immediately with halved limes.

for 4

SAY CHEESE

say cheese

PAGES 60/61 Cheeses at La Masseria, Stellenbosch.

ABOVE Floating taleggio.

OPPOSITE Making mozzarella.

Cheese-making started early on at the Cape, as the Dutch were renowned cheesemakers. They introduced their favourite sweetmilk and a cumin-flavoured cheese. Sweetmilk is very much an everyday household favourite, along with the popular English cheddar. Today cheeses are imported from everywhere, but the local cheese industry is growing rapidly, from Italian to French-style. Its success may be witnessed at the National Cheese Festival, a well-patronised event, recently introduced and now held annually. Under the English influence, cheese and biscuits ended the meal. But today, cheese and baguette could more often precede the dessert in the French way. Or a platter of pears and a choice of Italian cheeses. It's a Cape custom to serve cheese with preserves or 'konfyt', figs or watermelon in syrup – recipes first introduced by the French Huguenots.

cheese crisps

warm cheese salad

cheese tarts with rocket

twice-baked goat

cheese soufflés

green vegetable pancakes

with feta cheese sauce

hot spinach cheesecake

pancetta, spinach and

pasta timbales

goat cheese and

salad pizzas

parmesan potato pie

cappuccino cheesecake

cheese crisps

125 g gruyère cheese, grated
60 g soft butter
½ cup cake flour
a pinch cayenne pepper
a pinch salt

Mix all the ingredients together to form a dough. Roll into a sausage shape and wrap in greaseproof paper. Freeze until firm enough to slice.

Slice very thinly and bake at 190 °C for 5 minutes, or until golden, but watch carefully. Allow to cool slightly, then lift carefully onto a wire rack. Store in an airtight container.

warm cheese salad

a mix of greens for 4
4 garlic crostini (see page 32)

for the dressing, mix together
½ cup olive oil
2 Tbsp wine vinegar
salt and milled black pepper

for the cheeses
125 g ricotta cheese
1 Tbsp olive oil
2 Tbsp chopped fresh herbs
salt and milled black pepper
125 g soft goat cheese
olive oil for moistening
4 wedges camembert
whole-wheat cracker crumbs

Just before serving, mix the greens with the dressing and divide among 4 plates.

Pound the ricotta cheese with olive oil, herbs and seasoning. Shape into 8 balls and divide among the 4 salad plates.

Spread the crostini with goat cheese and drizzle with olive oil. Place on a foil-lined baking sheet. Dust the camembert wedges with crushed whole-wheat crackers and add to the baking sheet. Slide under a preheated grill for a few minutes or until the cheeses are hot and melting. Add to the salad plates and serve immediately.

for 4

cheese tarts with rocket

for the parmesan crust
1¼ cups cake flour
150 g cold unsalted butter
1¼ cups grated parmesan cheese

for the filling
1 punnet baby leeks, well washed
and thinly sliced
1 Tbsp unsalted butter
1 Tbsp olive oil
1 clove garlic, crushed
30 g rocket leaves, washed and torn
3 free-range eggs
250 g fresh mascarpone cheese
250 g feta cheese, crumbled
salt and milled black pepper

for garnishing
60 g rocket leaves, washed and dried
2 Tbsp olive oil
1 tsp red wine vinegar

To make the crust, sift the flour into a bowl. Grate in the butter and stir in the cheese. Rub lightly together with your fingertips to form a dough. Pat into six 12 cm loose-bottomed tart tins. Prick well and refrigerate while heating the oven to 200 °C. Bake for 8 minutes, or until pale golden. Allow to cool before adding the filling.

For the filling, gently cook the leeks in the heated butter and oil until very soft but still pale. Stir in the garlic. Remove from heat and allow to cool. Spoon the mixture into the baked tart shells. Add the rocket leaves in a layer, taking care to discard any stalks. Beat together the eggs and mascarpone, then stir in the crumbled feta and seasoning to taste. Spoon over the rocket. Bake at 200 °C for about 25 minutes, or until just set and golden. Remove from the tins.

Dress the rocket leaves with the olive oil and vinegar. Serve the tarts while still warm, topped with the dressed rocket leaves.

for 6

twice-baked goat cheese soufflés

40 g butter
40 g cake flour
1 cup warmed milk
250 g soft goat cheese, crumbled
3 free-range eggs, separated
salt and milled black pepper
1 cup fresh cream
6 Tbsp grated firm goat cheese

Melt the butter, then stir in the flour until smooth. Gradually whisk in the warmed milk. Bring to a boil, still whisking. Remove from heat and beat in the soft goat cheese. Beat in the egg yolks and seasoning to taste, then fold in the beaten egg whites.

Spoon into 6 well-buttered soufflé dishes and place in a baking pan of hot water. Bake at 220 °C for 15–20 minutes, or until puffed and set. To bake a second time, lift the cooled soufflés out of their dishes onto a buttered baking dish. Spoon over the cream and sprinkle generously with the firm goat cheese. Bake at 250 °C for 10 minutes, or until puffed and golden.

Serve as a starter or as a light main course with a mixed leaf salad.

for 4–6

green vegetable pancakes with feta cheese sauce

6 pancakes
½ cup thick cream
parmesan cheese for sprinkling
basil leaves for garnishing

for the filling
1 cup puréed steamed baby marrows or
cooked chopped spinach
2 free-range egg yolks
1 Tbsp shredded basil leaves
3 free-range egg whites

for the feta cheese sauce
30 g butter
2 Tbsp cake flour
1 cup warmed milk
100 g feta cheese, diced
salt and milled black pepper

First make the filling. Mix together the puréed green vegetable, egg yolks and basil, adding seasoning to taste. Fold in the stiffly beaten egg whites.

To make the cheese sauce, melt the butter and stir in the flour until smooth. Gradually stir in the milk and cook, still stirring, until thick and smooth. Stir in the feta and remove from the heat. Add a grinding of pepper and salt only if it needs it. If too thick, thin down with more milk.

To assemble and serve, place a generous spoonful of filling on each pancake and fold over. Arrange on a buttered baking sheet and smear with thick cream. Sprinkle with parmesan cheese.

Bake at 190 °C for 15 minutes, or until puffed and golden.

Serve immediately, ladling a spoonful of hot feta sauce over each pancake. Garnish with basil leaves.

for 6 as a starter, or 3 as a light main course with a salad

hot spinach cheesecake

for the crust
¼ cup melted butter
1 cup finely crushed savoury biscuits
¼ cup finely grated parmesan cheese

for the filling
1 onion, finely chopped
2 Tbsp butter
350 g spinach leaves, cooked
and chopped
250 g cream cheese
500 g ricotta cheese
1 cup sour cream
1 Tbsp cake flour
4 free-range eggs, beaten
salt and milled black pepper

Mix together all the ingredients for the crust. Press the mixture into a buttered 23 cm springform pan and chill for 30 minutes while preparing the filling.

To make the filling, gently soften the onion in the butter until pale golden. Allow to cool, then mix with the chopped spinach. Beat the cheeses with the cream, flour and eggs. Mix in the onion and spinach, and season to taste.

Pour the filling into the prepared pan and place on a baking sheet. Bake at 180 °C for 1 hour, or until golden brown and set. Leave to stand for 10–15 minutes before cutting into wedges.

for 8

Handmade cheese
Making mozzarella at La Masseria.

pancetta, spinach and pasta timbales

12 thin slices pancetta
12 Swiss chard leaves, well washed
250 g fresh thin pasta (tagliolini
or angel's hair)
4 free-range eggs
250 g mascarpone or
blue cheese and mascarpone mix
½ cup grated parmesan cheese
1 clove garlic, crushed
salt and milled black pepper

Coat a 12-muffin pan with non-stick cooking spray and line each one with a slice of pancetta.

Cut out the tough core from the Swiss chard leaves, then blanch in a large saucepan of boiling, salted water. Remove with tongs or a slotted spoon and cool.

Drop the pasta into the same saucepan of boiling water. Cook for about 3 minutes, until the pasta is just tender. Drain and cool.

Squeeze the leaves dry, then open out and place a leaf over the pancetta in each muffin pan. Beat the eggs with the mascarpone. Stir in the parmesan cheese, garlic and seasoning to taste. Mix with the pasta. Turn into the prepared muffin pans. Bake at 190 °C for about 30 minutes, or until slightly puffed, set and browned.

makes 12

goat cheese and salad pizzas

for the pizza base
1½ cups cake, bread or whole-wheat flour
½ tsp salt
1½ tsp instant yeast
⅔ cup warm water
1 Tbsp olive oil

for the topping
crushed garlic
125 g log chevin, thinly sliced
100 g firm goat cheese, grated
olive oil
milled black pepper
1 avocado, sliced
30 g rocket leaves

Sift the flour and salt into a bowl. Stir in the yeast, water and olive oil. Mix together to form a stiff dough, then turn out onto a floured board until smooth and elastic.

Cover the dough and leave to rise for approximately 20 minutes, or until well-risen and puffy. Punch down and knead again briefly. Leave to rest for about 5 minutes before rolling out, or simply stretching to fit a 30 cm pizza pan. Alternatively, form into a round and place on an oiled baking sheet. Brush with oil.

Smear the oiled pizza base with crushed garlic. Add the sliced chevin, then sprinkle with the grated cheese. Drizzle with a little oil and add a grinding of black pepper.

Meanwhile, preheat the oven to a fierce 240 °C and bake, near the bottom of the oven, for 10–15 minutes, until the base is cooked and starting to catch and the cheese is melting.

Remove and top with sliced avocado and a tuft of rocket leaves moistened with olive oil. Add salt and black pepper to taste and serve immediately.

for 1–2 as a meal, or 6–8 as an appetiser

parmesan potato pie

1 kg Mediterranean-style potatoes, peeled
½ cup milk
2 free-range eggs, beaten
½ cup grated parmesan cheese
grated nutmeg
salt and milled black pepper
1–2 Tbsp dried home-made breadcrumbs
olive oil for drizzling

Cut the potatoes into large chunks and boil until tender. Drain and dry the potatoes on the stove. Pour the milk into the pot with the potatoes and allow to warm through. Mash vigorously with a potato masher until smooth. Mix in the beaten eggs, ¼ cup grated parmesan cheese, nutmeg and seasoning to taste.

Turn into a shallow, oiled baking tin and smooth the surface with a spatula. Sprinkle with the remaining parmesan cheese and breadcrumbs and drizzle with oil. Bake at 200 °C for 15–20 minutes or until golden. Cut into squares for serving.

Serve as a side dish with roast meats or fish, along with a green salad.

for 6–8

cappuccino cheesecake

for the crust
1½ cups sweet biscuit crumbs
1 tsp ground cinnamon
⅓–½ cup melted butter

Mix together all the ingredients for the crust. Press onto the bottom and halfway up the sides of a 23 cm springform pan, then refrigerate while preparing the filling.

for the filling
5 free-range eggs
750 g creamed cottage cheese
1 cup castor sugar
⅓ cup very strong black coffee, cooled

To make the filling, beat all the ingredients together. Place the prepared springform pan on a baking sheet. Pour in the filling and bake at 160 °C for 50 minutes, or until just set. First cool, then refrigerate overnight.

for the topping
1 cup fresh cream, whipped
sifted cocoa and ground cinnamon

As near to serving as possible, remove the cheesecake from the pan. Put onto a plate and top with the whipped cream. Sprinkle with sifted cocoa and cinnamon.

for 8–10

HOT KOESIESTERS
SUNDAYS

PIES
STEAK & KIDNEY
PEPPER STEAK
STEAK
CHIC. & MUSHROOM
CURRY MINCE
CORNISH - PASTY

ROSE
CORNER CAFE

"LEKKEK
WARM
WORSIES
ELKE DONDERDAG!

HOT PIES
and
SAMOOSAS
Daily

PHONECARD
SOLD HERE

Ola
Ice Crea

SPICE IS NICE

spiced lentil dip

goat cheese and
coriander pesto samoosas

**spiced pumpkin and
tomato soup**

fish curry

**spiced fish rice
with dukkah**

chicken curry

**chicken tagine with
chickpeas and dates**

spiced roast lamb with
eggplant and pilaf

**lamb bobotie with
basmati rice and chilli jam**

braised veal shin with
steamed vegetables
and couscous

**spiced date and
coconut pancakes**

chocolate ginger cake

PAGES 78/79 Rose Corner Café, Bo-Kaap.

ABOVE Bo-Kaap, Cape Town.

Spice was the very reason for the start of Cape Town. A half-way refreshment station was established here in 1652 to provide for the sailors journeying between the East and Holland, taking the lucrative spices back home and so swelling the coffers of the powerful Dutch East India Company (V.O.C.). Once slaves from Indonesia arrived later in the century, spiced dishes were introduced to the Dutch table. These Malay women were excellent cooks, and their contribution is an important part of the local cuisine. A favourite dish is bobotie, a curried mince with a sunshine yellow spiced savoury custard topping, that was served on Monday from the leftover Sunday roast lamb that the Dutch families habitually enjoyed. Rice and potatoes often sat side by side with traditional dishes, because the Northern European Dutch loved their potatoes, and the Malay slaves couldn't do without rice at every meal, and they grew fond of each other's staples.

spiced lentil dip

½ cup brown lentils
½ cup red lentils
3 Tbsp olive oil
1 onion, chopped
2 fat cloves garlic, crushed
1 tsp turmeric
1 tsp ground cumin
½ cup coriander leaves,
washed and dried
1 Tbsp fresh lemon juice
½ tsp chilli powder
salt to taste

Soak the lentils in cold water for
20–30 minutes. Skim off any gritty bits
and drain. Cook for about 30 minutes,
or until tender. Drain.

Heat the oil in a wide, heavy pan.
Add the onion and cook gently until
softened but not browned. Stir in the garlic,
turmeric and cumin until fragrant. Process
or blend together with the lentils, coriander,
lemon juice and chilli powder until smooth.
Add salt to taste. Store in the refrigerator.

for serving
crisp poppadums

Serve at room temperature with crisply fried
poppadums for dipping.

for 8

goat cheese and coriander pesto samoosas

150 g soft goat cheese
4 sheets fresh phyllo pastry or ready-cut
samoosa pastry strips
melted unsalted butter
vegetable oil for frying

for the coriander pesto
1 cup coriander leaves, washed and dried
2 fresh green chillies, seeded
and chopped
2 cloves garlic, crushed
2 Tbsp toasted sunflower seeds
¼ cup olive oil
salt to taste

for the yoghurt sauce
½ cup thick Greek yoghurt
2 Tbsp chopped mango chutney
1 Tbsp chopped lime pickle

First make the pesto. Pound together all the pesto ingredients and set aside.

To make the filling, mix the goat cheese with the pesto.

Cut each sheet of pastry across (not lengthwise) into six strips. Brush both sides with melted butter. For each samoosa, place 1 tsp of filling in one corner. Fold over to form a triangle, pressing the edges together. Continue folding over, bottom corner towards the opposite side, to form triangular pastries. Press the edges together and seal with melted butter.

If more convenient, prepare ahead and refrigerate the pastries, covered with plastic clingfilm.

Fry the pastries in hot vegetable oil until crisp and golden. Mix together the ingredients for the yoghurt sauce and serve with the hot samoosas.

makes 24 pastries

spiced pumpkin and tomato soup

1 large onion, chopped
2 Tbsp sunflower oil
1 tsp curry powder
1 fat clove garlic, crushed
1 kg peeled and diced pumpkin
5 cups chicken or vegetable stock
½–1 cup buttermilk or coconut milk
1 x 410 g can Indian-style
chopped tomatoes
salt and milled black pepper

for serving
garam masala
coriander leaves

Gently cook the onion in the oil with a little salt until softened but not browned. If necessary add a little water. Stir in the curry powder and garlic, then add the diced pumpkin, cover and cook for about 10 minutes. Pour in the stock, cover and simmer for about 30 minutes, or until the pumpkin is tender.

Purée with an electric hand-held blender until smooth. If serving cold, add enough buttermilk to make a suitable consistency. Stir in the tomatoes but do not purée. Check seasoning and refrigerate.

If serving hot, reheat gently with coconut milk instead of the buttermilk, and the tomatoes. Serve, sprinkled with garam masala and coriander leaves. Put out a pile of crisp poppadums as an accompaniment.

for 8

fish curry

1 kg fresh fish, skinned and filletted
50 g butter
1 Tbsp sunflower oil
3 onions, thinly sliced
chunk of fresh root ginger, peeled and grated
3 cloves garlic, crushed
3 ripe red tomatoes, skinned and finely chopped
1–2 sticks cinnamon
6 cardamom pods, cracked
1 Tbsp ground turmeric
1 Tbsp curry powder or fish masala
4 medium potatoes, peeled, parboiled and quartered
salt
1 tsp garam masala
handful of coriander leaves, chopped

Cut the fish into chunks and set aside.

Heat the butter and oil and cook the onions gently for about 10 minutes, or until softened but still pale. Stir in the fish, ginger and garlic. Stir in the tomatoes, cinnamon, cardamom, turmeric, curry powder, potatoes and some salt. Cover and simmer for 10 minutes, adding a little water if necessary, until the fish is just cooked through and the potatoes are tender.

Stir in the garam masala and the chopped coriander. Check seasoning.

Serve with lots of steamed basmati rice, a fruity chutney and a sharp lime pickle. Add a bowl of puréed spinach on the side.

for 4–6

Cape pickled fish

Gently cook 3 thinly sliced onions in 2 Tbsp oil until softened and pale golden. Add 1 Tbsp curry powder and 1 tsp turmeric and stir for 1–2 minutes. Add 1½ cups vinegar, ½ cup water, 2 Tbsp sugar, 3 bay leaves, 8 peppercorns and 6 allspice. Bring to the boil, then simmer until the onions are tender. Pour the hot mixture over the fish (about 1 kg freshly fried, leftover roasted, or barbecued). Once cooled, refrigerate for a few days before serving.

for 6

spiced fish rice with dukkah

1–2 onions, chopped
3–4 Tbsp sunflower oil
2 tsp ground cumin
2 tsp ground coriander
1–2 fresh chillies, chopped
2–3 fat cloves garlic, crushed
2 cups basmati rice
2 cups fish stock
2 cups water
1 bay leaf
1 stick cinnamon
1 fish head and bones
1 tsp salt
2–3 hard-boiled free-range eggs, chopped
2–3 Tbsp dukkah for sprinkling
coriander leaves

Gently soften the onion in hot oil. Stir in the cumin and coriander, then the chilli, garlic and rice. Stir for 1–2 minutes, then pour in the stock and water. Add the bay leaf, cinnamon, fish head and bones, and salt.

Bring to a simmer, then reduce heat and cook for about 15 minutes, or until the rice is tender and the liquid absorbed. Once cool, remove bits of fish from the head and bones and add to the rice. Check seasoning.

Turn onto a platter and sprinkle with egg and dukkah and tuck in coriander leaves. Serve warm or at room temperature.

for 6–8

For oven roasting I like to use the whole fillets of a large fish, easy to cook, and easy to serve. I use the head and bones for flavouring basmati rice. But you could, of course, make this dish simply using 4 cups fish stock, or even chicken or vegetable. You'll find dukkah, a Middle Eastern mix of seeds and nuts, at good food shops. I included a recipe in my last cookbook, *The Monday to Sunday Cookbook* (Struik).

chicken curry

1 kg free-range chicken pieces
2 Tbsp sunflower oil
2 onions, chopped
3 sticks cinnamon
3 cardamom pods, cracked
1 fat clove garlic, crushed
1 chunk root ginger, peeled and grated
3 ripe red tomatoes, skinned and chopped
2 Tbsp mild curry powder or
chicken masala
6 curry leaves
salt
1 cup water or coconut milk
4 medium potatoes, peeled and cubed
fresh coriander leaves

Wash the chicken pieces. Heat the oil in a heavy saucepan and braise the onions slowly together with the cinnamon and cardamom, for about 10 minutes. Add the chicken pieces, garlic and ginger. Cover and cook for about 20 minutes, stirring now and again, until a good colour.

Add the tomatoes, curry powder or masala and curry leaves, and mix together well. Add some salt and pour in the water or coconut milk.

Stir in the potatoes and cook gently for about 30 minutes or until everything is tender. Stir in a good handful of chopped coriander leaves and check seasoning.

Serve with steamed basmati rice, or roti breads, a sweet chutney and a sharp mango pickle. Make a tomato sambal to go with it: a mix of chopped tomato, chopped onion and fresh chilli, a little vinegar, and salt and pepper. Or a bowl of cool cucumber, chopped and mixed with yoghurt and mint, fresh or dried.

for 4–6

Street food in the Bo-Kaap
Barbecued Iraqi butterflied chicken.

Best rotis in town
Monica Zoyi serving rotis and curries at
Zorina's Café, Loop Street, Cape Town.

chicken tagine with chickpeas and dates

8 free-range chicken thighs
2 Tbsp olive oil
salt and milled black pepper
2 large onions, thinly sliced
1 tsp ground cinnamon
1 tsp ground ginger
¼ tsp saffron
1 cup water
2 lemons
200 g dates, fresh or dried
1 can chickpeas, drained and rinsed
a handful of coriander leaves, chopped

for serving
rose water
toasted sesame seeds
toasted flaked almonds
couscous
chilli jam

Wash and dry the chicken pieces. Heat oil in a suitable saucepan. Add chicken, in batches if necessary, and brown all over. Remove and season.

Add the onion to the fat in the saucepan. Cook gently, covered, for about 15 minutes until very soft but still pale. Stir in cinnamon, ginger and saffron.

Return chicken to saucepan, pour in water and juice of 1 lemon. Pour boiling water over the second lemon, drain and slice thinly. Add to the chicken. Cover and simmer for about 40 minutes, or until chicken is very tender.

Add dates and chickpeas. Simmer for a further 10 minutes, until heated through. Stir in the coriander leaves. Check seasoning.

Sprinkle with rose water, toasted sesame seeds and almond flakes.

Serve with hot couscous (cooked according to packet directions). Pass around chilli jam.

for 4–8

Tagine, a slowly simmered stew, takes its name from the shallow earthernware braising utensil with a conical cover in which it is traditionally cooked in Morocco.

spiced roast lamb with eggplant and pilaf

2 kg leg of lamb
4 tsp ground cumin
2 tsp ground coriander
2 tsp dried oregano
4 cloves garlic, crushed
olive oil
salt and milled black pepper
2 large onions, thinly sliced
1 cup stock or water
1 cup dry red wine
2 large eggplants, thinly sliced lengthwise

for the pilaf
2 Tbsp olive oil
2 cups rice
1 tsp ground cumin
1 x 410 g can chopped tomatoes
1 clove garlic, crushed
2 cups stock or water
¼–⅓ cup currants
½ tsp dried oregano
1 tsp salt
¼ cup pinenuts
fresh oregano, for garnishing

Trim any excess fat from lamb.

Make a paste with spices, oregano, garlic, ¼ cup olive oil and some seasoning. Smear all over the lamb. Place in a lightly oiled roasting pan on a bed of onions. Roast, uncovered, at 180 °C for 1½ hours, then pour over the stock and wine and roast for another 30 minutes, or until very tender.

Arrange the eggplant in a single layer on oiled baking sheets. Season and brush with olive oil. Bake at 180 °C for 15 minutes, or until tender.

To make the pilaf, gently heat the oil in a suitable casserole. Stir in rice for 1–2 minutes, until translucent but not browned. Stir in cumin, then the tomatoes and cook gently for about 5 minutes.

Stir in the garlic, stock, currants, oregano and salt. Bring to a bubble, then cover tightly and bake at 180 °C for about 30 minutes, or until liquid is absorbed and the rice is tender. Check seasoning. Turn onto a platter and sprinkle with the toasted pinenuts.

To serve, carve lamb thinly and serve with eggplant and pilaf, garnished with fresh oregano. Pass around the pan juices.

for 6

lamb bobotie
with basmati rice and chilli jam

2 onions, sliced
2 Tbsp sunflower oil or butter
1 kg lean lamb mince
¼ cup seedless raisins
¼ cup finely chopped dried apricots
2 slices bread, cubed and with
crusts removed
1¼ cups buttermilk
3 free-range eggs
1 apple, peeled and grated
¼ cup toasted flaked almonds
2 Tbsp apricot jam
1 Tbsp curry powder
2 Tbsp fresh lemon juice
salt and milled black pepper
6 fresh lemon or bay leaves
¼ tsp turmeric

for serving
steamed basmati rice and chilli jam

I also make a fish bobotie using minced fresh hake instead of the lamb.

Gently cook the onion in the heated oil or butter until soft and pale golden. Stir in the meat (or fish), using a large fork to break up any lumps. As soon as the meat changes colour, remove from the heat.

Pour boiling water over the raisins and apricots. Mix the bread with 1 cup buttermilk and 1 beaten egg, mashing together with a fork. Add the drained dried fruits, apple, almonds, jam, curry powder, lemon juice and salt and pepper to taste. Mix well together, then lightly mix in the meat mixture, using the fork. Check seasoning.

Turn into a suitably sized, oiled baking dish and spread evenly. Curl leaves and tuck into the mixture. Bake uncovered at 180 °C for 30 minutes.

Remove from oven and pour over a topping made from beating the remaining buttermilk with the remaining 2 eggs and turmeric. Return to the oven for 10 minutes, or until the topping is set.

for 6

braised veal shin with steamed vegetables and couscous

12 pieces thick veal shin
flour for dusting
oil for frying
salt and milled black pepper
1 cup dry red wine
4 cups hot beef stock
a pinch saffron
2 Tbsp tomato paste
1 tsp harissa paste
3–4 sticks cinnamon
2 onions, peeled and chopped
250 g butternut squash, peeled and chopped
2 carrots, peeled and chopped
2 turnips, peeled and chopped
2 baby marrows, chopped
3 fat cloves garlic, crushed
a few strips orange peel
500 g couscous, cooked
a handful fresh coriander leaves

vegetables for steaming
250 g whole baby carrots
250 g baby turnips, cut into wedges
250 g butternut squash, peeled and cubed
250 g baby marrows, sliced
1 red or yellow pepper, seeded and sliced

Pat the meat quite dry. Dust with flour and fry in a minimum of oil – not too many pieces at a time – until nicely browned all over. Set aside and season.

Pour the wine into a casserole and bring to a bubble. Return the browned meat to the casserole and add the rest of the ingredients, except the couscous, coriander and vegetables for steaming. Bring to a bubble on top of the stove, then cover tightly and bake at 160 °C for 2 hours, or until meltingly tender. Remove the meat and keep warm. Remove the vegetable pieces with a slotted spoon and purée with a hand blender.

Meanwhile, reduce the cooking liquid on the stove until lightly thickened, then stir in the puréed vegetables to make a rich thick sauce. Check seasoning.

Steam the remaining vegetables until done.

To serve, turn hot couscous onto a platter. Spoon over the meat and half the sauce, then top with the steamed vegetables and fresh coriander leaves. Pass around the rest of the sauce and some harissa paste at the table.

for 6–8

spiced date and coconut pancakes

for the pancakes

¾ cup stone-ground white flour

a pinch salt

3 free-range eggs

1 cup buttermilk

1 Tbsp sunflower oil

butter for frying

for the filling

250 g soft pitted dates, chopped

½ cup desiccated coconut

½ cup coconut cream

1 or 2 sticks cinnamon

2 cracked cardamom pods

Beat the pancake ingredients together, strain into a jug and allow to rest in the refrigerator for about 1 hour. Give it a whisk, and if it's too thick (it should be the consistency of pouring cream), thin down with a little water.

Cook the batter in a medium-sized pan, well heated and buttered, to make approximately 10 pancakes.

Gently cook the filling ingredients together for 5–10 minutes to make a thick paste. Discard the spices.

To assemble, spread the pancakes generously with the date paste. Roll or fold and serve immediately, sprinkled with ground cinnamon. Or arrange in a buttered baking dish. Pour over coconut cream and bake at 190 °C for 10–15 minutes, or until heated through. Dust with ground cinnamon.

for 4–6

chocolate ginger cake

¾ cup boiling water
½ cup cocoa powder
1¾ cups cake flour
1¾ cups sugar
1½ tsp bicarbonate of soda
1 tsp salt
1 tsp ground ginger
½ cup sunflower oil
7 free-range eggs, separated
½ tsp cream of tartar
½ cup chopped ginger preserve

for the chocolate glaze
100 g dark chocolate, broken into bits
¼ cup fresh cream

for decorating
ginger preserve

Mix the boiling water and cocoa, and set aside to cool.

Sift the flour, sugar, bicarbonate of soda, salt and ground ginger together. Make a well in the centre of the dry ingredients and add the oil, egg yolks and cocoa mixture. Beat until very smooth.

Beat the egg whites and cream of tartar together until very stiff. Pour the egg yolk mixture in a thin stream over the beaten egg whites, gently folding in with a spatula until well blended. Fold in the chopped ginger preserve.

Pour into an ungreased 25 cm x 10 cm tube pan. Bake at 160 °C for 55 minutes, then increase the heat to 180 °C and bake for a further 10–15 minutes. Invert the cake and let it hang over the neck of a funnel or bottle, until quite cold. Gently remove from the tin with a metal spatula.

To make the glaze, gently heat the chocolate and cream together until melted. Mix until smooth. Allow to cool for 1–2 minutes and pour over the cake. Decorate with ginger preserve. Serve with whipped cream.

for 12

BETWEEN THE VINES

between the vines

It is recorded that on 2 February 1659 wine was made for the first time in the Cape. Jan van Riebeeck was delighted with the way grapes flourished. Varieties from all over the world were successfully grown, and Van Riebeeck himself developed the still much-loved hanepoot grape, with its honey-sweet distinctive flavour. The expertise of both Simon van der Stel, who came as governor in 1679, and the French Huguenots, in 1688, did much to improve the quality of wine. Visitors to the Cape praised the Constantia wines. One reads of their popularity in England in the novels of Jane Austen, and Napoleon is said to have enjoyed Constantia wine during his exile on St Helena. Today South African wines hold their own internationally, winning awards and increasing export orders.

PAGES 100/101 Buitenverwachting, Constantia. The Cape is considered one of the most beautiful vineyard areas in the world.

OPPOSITE A bunch of Pinot Noir grapes.

braised fish with red wine and mushrooms

braised chicken thighs with red wine, sun-dried tomatoes and balsamic vinegar

roast duck with sultana grapes and hanepoot sauce

guinea fowl and red cabbage casserole

roast quails with baked pumpkin polenta

ostrich steaks with chicken livers, shallots and port wine

pappardelle with venison and mushrooms

braised lamb shanks with pinotage

cape grape cake

grape tart

nectarines in rosé wine syrup

baked whole plums in sweet wine

pink champagne jellies

braised fish with red wine and mushrooms

750 g–1 kg filletted fish (yellowtail or
fresh tuna)
3 Tbsp olive oil
1 bunch leeks, thinly sliced
2 sticks celery, finely chopped
2 carrots, finely chopped
1 cup fish stock
1 cup dry red wine
2 Tbsp tomato paste
2 fat cloves garlic, crushed
1 bunch herbs (rosemary sprig, thyme
and a bay leaf)
salt and milled black pepper
250–300 g open brown mushrooms,
thickly sliced
butter for frying

for garnishing
snipped chives

for serving
steamed potatoes
garlic-orange mayonnaise

for the garlic-orange mayonnaise
zest of 1 bright orange
1 free-range egg
1 clove garlic, crushed
1 tsp red wine vinegar
2 Tbsp fresh orange juice
salt and milled black pepper
1½ cups sunflower oil

Rinse and dry the fish. Cut into fairly large chunks. Heat the oil in a suitably heavy casserole and add the leeks, celery and carrots. Cook very gently until softened but not browned. Increase the heat and add the fish. Cook, stirring, for a few minutes. Stir in the stock, red wine, tomato paste, crushed garlic and herbs. Cook fiercely for about 5 minutes until the fish is just cooked and still moist, and the sauce reduced. Add seasoning to taste.

In a separate pan, fry the mushrooms in a minimum of hot butter, season lightly and add to the casserole. Check seasoning, sprinkle with chives and serve in soup bowls with steamed potatoes and a dab of garlic-orange mayonnaise.

To make the garlic-orange mayonnaise, place the zest in a bowl and pour over boiling water. In a food processor, or using a hand blender, whizz the egg with the garlic, vinegar, orange juice, drained zest and some seasoning. Gradually add the oil (adding more if necessary) and beat until thick and smooth. Check seasoning.

for 4–6

braised chicken thighs with red wine, sun-dried tomatoes and balsamic vinegar

16–18 chicken thigh portions (about 2 kg)
2 Tbsp olive oil
2 onions, thinly sliced
salt and milled black pepper
2–3 cloves garlic, crushed
¼ cup shredded basil leaves or
2 tsp dried origanum
125 g sun-dried tomatoes
3 cups chicken stock
1 cup dry red wine
¼ cup balsamic vinegar

for garnishing
fresh basil leaves or finely chopped parsley

Trim any excess fat from the chicken. Wash and dry well.

Heat the oil in a heavy, ovenproof casserole and brown the chicken over a medium-high heat in 3–4 batches. Arrange each batch in a single layer, skin-side down, until nicely browned. Turn and briefly brown the other side. Remove with a slotted spoon and season lightly.

Reduce the heat and add the onions and a little seasoning. Cook gently for 5–10 minutes or until very soft but not browned. If necessary add small amounts of water to prevent catching. Stir in the garlic, then return the chicken to the casserole. Stir in the herbs and tomatoes. Pour in the stock and wine, and bring to a bubble. Place a sheet of oiled greaseproof paper directly on the surface and cover with the lid. Place in the oven at 160 °C and bake for about 1 hour, or until the chicken is very tender. Remove and allow to cool. Refrigerate overnight.

Before reheating the chicken, remove any congealed fat from the surface. Bring to a simmer on top of the stove. Check seasoning. If there seems to be too much liquid, remove the chicken pieces with a slotted spoon and reduce the liquid until slightly thickened. Stir in the balsamic vinegar (and chicken pieces, if necessary). Reheat on top of the stove or in the oven at 160 °C for 20–30 minutes. Check seasoning once more.

Serve with hot, cooked small pasta, sprinkled with shredded basil or chopped parsley.

for 8

roast duck with
sultana grapes and hanepoot sauce

1 duck (about 2 kg)
salt and milled black pepper
1 onion, peeled and quartered
a few sprigs each celery and parsley
1 cup sultana grapes

for the duck stock
1 onion, 1 carrot and 1 stick celery, all
roughly chopped
oil
giblets and wing tips (from duck)
2 cups water
a few sprigs parsley

for the sauce
4 Tbsp runny honey
6 Tbsp wine vinegar
1 cup duck stock
2 Tbsp cornflour
4 Tbsp brandy
1 cup unsweetened hanepoot grape juice
1 cup sweet hanepoot wine

Remove any visible fat from the duck. Prick well. Season inside and out. Fill the cavity with onion and herbs. Place the bird breast-side up on an oiled rack in a roasting pan. Pour water into the bottom of the pan to prevent smoking. Roast at 220 °C for 30 minutes, then reduce to 190 °C. Turn the duck over, prick again and roast for 1 hour.

Remove from the oven and drain the fat and water. This may be prepared in advance.

About 45 minutes before serving, quarter the duck, discarding the backbone and flavourings, and place it skin-side up in an ovenproof dish. Pour over sauce and roast at 200 °C for 30 minutes, basting, until the meat is tender and the skin golden and crisp. Add grapes 5–10 minutes before cooking time ends.

For the stock, soften the vegetables in a little oil. Add the giblets and wing tips, and cook until nicely browned. Add the remaining ingredients. Cover and simmer gently for 1 hour. Strain and set aside. Check seasoning.

For the sauce, boil honey and vinegar in a heavy saucepan until syrupy. Remove from heat and add stock, stirring constantly. Mix the cornflour and brandy to a smooth paste and stir into the sauce. Still stirring, simmer until the sauce thickens. Stir in the grape juice and wine and bring to the boil. Reduce slightly. Add seasoning to taste. Check that the sauce is pleasantly sweet and sour, adding lemon juice, if necessary.

for 4

guinea fowl and red cabbage casserole

Try pheasant when in season, as a change from guinea fowl.

1 guinea fowl with giblets, cleaned
and trimmed
3 Tbsp olive oil
salt and milled black pepper
4 rashers rindless streaky bacon, chopped
1 onion, finely chopped
2 carrots, finely chopped
2 sticks celery, finely chopped
3 or 4 sprigs parsley, chopped
3 or 4 sprigs thyme, chopped
2 cloves garlic, crushed
1 red cabbage, cored and cut into wedges
1 bay leaf
1 cup dry red wine
2 cups chicken stock
grated nutmeg
2 or 3 juniper berries or allspice
1 stick cinnamon
2 Tbsp brown sugar
2 Tbsp red wine vinegar
2 Tbsp butter

for serving
roasted potatoes

for garnishing
fresh thyme

Remove the backbone of the bird and chop into 2 or 3 pieces. Cut the bird into 4 portions and brown in oil in a heavy casserole. Remove and season. Brown the liver, backbone pieces and giblets, remove and set aside.

Add bacon, vegetables and herbs to the casserole and cook, stirring now and again, until very soft, adding a little more oil if necessary. Stir in the garlic. Return the browned portions and giblets to casserole. Add cabbage wedges (packing in tightly), bay leaf and a little seasoning. Pour over wine and stock. Add the spices. Sprinkle the sugar and vinegar over the cabbage. Dot cabbage with butter, cover tightly and bake at 190 °C for about 1 hour or until tender. Remove giblets and backbone bits, and discard along with whole spices.

Remove bird and cabbage to heated platter and keep warm. Add chopped liver to sauce. Purée sauce and reduce over a high heat to a suitable consistency. Check seasoning. Spoon over portions. Serve with roasted potatoes and garnish with thyme.

for 2–4

roast quails with baked pumpkin polenta

8 oven-ready quails
salt and milled black pepper
fresh sage leaves
8 bay leaves
1 onion, thinly sliced
2–4 cloves garlic, smashed
olive oil
runny honey
½ cup chicken stock
½ cup dry wine

for serving
baked pumpkin polenta
rocket leaves

Wash the quails and dry very well. Season inside and out and stuff each one with fresh sage leaves, a bay leaf, some thinly sliced onion and garlic. Rub with olive oil and arrange in an oiled roasting pan, breast-side up. Roast at 230 °C for 15 minutes.

Drizzle with a little honey and pour over the stock and wine. Roast for a further 10–15 minutes, basting once or twice, or until nicely browned and tender. Serve with pumpkin polenta and rocket leaves.

for the baked pumpkin polenta
500 g peeled and chopped pumpkin
3 cups chicken stock
grated nutmeg
salt and milled black pepper
1 cup instant polenta
olive oil

Simmer the pumpkin in the stock with a grating of nutmeg and some seasoning, covered, until tender. Drain, but reserve the stock to make the polenta.

Make up the polenta according to packet instructions. Mash the pumpkin and mix together with the cooked polenta. Check seasoning and turn into an oiled baking pan. Drizzle with olive oil. Bake at 230 °C for about 30 minutes, or until golden.

for 4–6

Selected for pressing
Freshly picked grapes at Buitenverwachting.

ostrich steaks with chicken livers, shallots and port wine

4 portions ostrich fillet or steaks
olive oil
200 g shallots
¼ cup seedless raisins
salt and milled black pepper
250 g chicken livers (or portabellini
mushrooms, if you prefer)
1 cup chicken stock
½ cup port wine
whole chives for garnishing

for serving
butternut mash and steamed greens

Prime cuts of ostrich, like beef fillet, are juicy and tasty. The meat is deep red in colour and less firm than beef. Cook it fast, seared on top of the stove. Anything slower, like oven roasting, dries it out.

Pat the meat dry, then moisten with oil. Pour boiling water over the shallots and, when cool enough to handle, drain and peel. Pour boiling water over the raisins and leave to soak, but leave them out if using mushrooms.

Sear the oiled steaks in a hot, non-stick pan to brown on both sides. Remove and season. Add a little oil, as well as the well-dried chicken livers (or sliced portabellini mushrooms) and brown briskly. Remove and season lightly.

Add a little more oil and the shallots. Brown all over. Add the stock. Simmer for about 10 minutes or until the shallots are very tender, adding more stock if necessary. Add the drained raisins (if using) and port, and simmer until suitably reduced.

Return the steaks and chicken livers (or mushrooms) to the pan and heat through. Serve garnished with chives.

for 4

pappardelle with venison and mushrooms

500 g pappardelle

for the sauce
25 g dried porcini mushrooms
125 g rindless bacon
2 Tbsp olive oil
1 onion, chopped
1 kg venison goulash (or any cubed braising cut)
salt and milled black pepper
1 cup beef stock
2 cups dry red wine
1 bay leaf
a few sprigs parsley and thyme
1 clove garlic, crushed
½ cup sour cream
250 g medium open brown mushrooms
1 Tbsp unsalted butter
chopped parsley

Soak the dried mushrooms in 1 cup warm or boiling water for 20–30 minutes.

In a heavy casserole, heat the chopped bacon until the fat runs. Add half the oil and the onion and cook gently until softened but not browned. Remove with a slotted spoon and set aside.

Add the rest of the oil and brown the meat in batches, adding a little more oil if needed. Lightly season each batch. Return the browned meat, bacon and onion to the casserole. Pour in the stock and wine, add the herbs, garlic, strained mushroom liquid, soaked mushrooms and a little seasoning. Bring to a bubble, then cover the meat with a sheet of oiled greaseproof paper and a tight lid and bake at 160 °C for 1¼ hours or until the meat is very tender.

Remove the meat and keep warm while reducing the liquid on top of the stove until slightly thickened. Beat in the cream and allow to heat through. Check seasoning.

Meanwhile, stir-fry the brown mushrooms in the hot butter until just cooked, then season lightly. Turn the just cooked, drained pasta onto a heated platter. Spoon the meat over it, pour over the sauce, then top with the fried mushrooms and lots of chopped parsley.

for 4–6

Pappardelle are very wide noodles, generally served with game.

braised lamb shanks with pinotage

Pinotage is South Africa's 'own' grape variety –
a cross between Cinsaut and Pinot Noir.

8 lamb shanks

¼ cup olive oil

salt and milled black pepper

2 onions, thinly sliced

1 or 2 carrots, finely chopped

1 or 2 sticks celery, finely chopped

1 or 2 sprigs rosemary

1 stick cinnamon

3 cups beef or chicken stock

2 cloves garlic, crushed

1 piece dried naartjie peel

2 cups pinotage

¼ cup brown sugar

½ cup red wine vinegar

1 or 2 Tbsp tomato paste

1 cup seedless raisins, soaked overnight in
brandy to cover

fresh herbs for garnishing

Wipe the meat with a damp, clean cloth, then pat dry. Using a heavy casserole, brown the meat in batches in 2 Tbsp oil. Remove and season lightly.

Reduce heat, pour off the fat, and add the remaining oil, onions, carrots, celery, rosemary and cinnamon. Cook gently for 10–15 minutes, or until the vegetables are soft and pale golden, adding a little stock if necessary. Stir in the garlic and naartjie peel. Pour in the wine and bring to a bubble. Allow to boil and reduce slightly. In a small saucepan stir the sugar with 2 Tbsp water until dissolved. Allow to boil for barely a minute until slightly syrupy, then remove from heat and add the vinegar.

Return the lamb and any accumulated juices to the casserole. Add the stock, tomato paste and caramel-vinegar mixture and bring to a simmer. If necessary add more wine or stock to cover. Cover with a sheet of oiled greaseproof paper and the lid and bake at 160 °C for 1½ hours. Add the brandied raisins and cook, covered, for another 30 minutes, or until the meat is meltingly tender.

Remove the lamb and keep warm. Discard the rosemary, cinnamon and peel. Reduce the cooking liquids on the stove top, to intensify the flavour. Taste for seasoning and sweet-sour balance. Adjust if necessary. Return the lamb to the casserole and reheat gently before serving. Garnish with herbs. Serve with mashed sweet potatoes (enriched with butter and flavoured with orange juice) and a mix of steamed greens.

for 8

cape grape cake

1½ cups cake flour
1 tsp baking powder
1 tsp salt
¼ tsp bicarbonate of soda
¾ cup castor sugar
100 g unsalted butter, at room temperature
3 Tbsp best olive oil
2 free-range eggs
1 tsp vanilla essence
1 cup sweet hanepoot wine
rind of 1 lemon and 1 orange, grated
1½ cups seedless grapes

for topping
2 Tbsp unsalted butter
2 Tbsp sugar

Sift flour together with the baking powder, salt and bicarbonate of soda. Beat the sugar with the butter and oil until pale and creamy. Beat in the eggs. Add the vanilla. Gently beat in the flour mixture alternately with the wine until just smooth. Add the rind. Turn into a 23 cm springform pan coated with non-stick cooking spray. Smooth the top and sprinkle with the grapes. Bake at 200 °C for 20 minutes, or until the top is set.

Dot with remaining butter and sprinkle with remaining sugar. Bake for a further 20 minutes or until golden and cooked through when tested. Allow to cool for about 20 minutes before removing. Serve at room temperature.

for 8

Moist and winey, the cake keeps well. Usually I can't wait, and love a still-warm wedge with a glass of chilled hanepoot wine.

grape tart

for the pastry
1 x 20 cm fully baked tart shell

for the custard
3 Tbsp sugar
1 Tbsp cornflour
1 cup milk
2 tsp butter
2 free-range egg yolks
1 Tbsp sweet hanepoot wine
½ cup fresh cream, whipped

for topping
2 cups seedless grapes

for glazing
2 Tbsp melted grape, apple or quince jelly

for serving
serve on fresh vine leaves

For the custard, mix the sugar and cornflour together in a saucepan. Gradually add milk and stir until smooth. Add the butter. Cook, stirring all the time, until the mixture begins to boil. Allow to boil for 1 minute, then remove from heat.

Warm the egg yolks by mixing with a little of the hot mixture. Stir into the rest of the hot mixture. Cook, stirring constantly, until the mixture comes to the boil. Immediately remove from heat and stir in the wine. Strain and allow to cool. Place a piece of greaseproof paper directly on the surface to prevent a skin forming.

Fold the whipped cream into the cooled custard, then refrigerate until using.

To assemble, fill the cooled tart shell with the custard filling, top with grapes and glaze with melted grape jelly.

for 6

On sale at a roadside kiosk
Honey-sweet, freshly picked hanepoot grapes from Constantia Uitsig are much in demand during their short season.

nectarines in rosé wine syrup

6 perfect ripe nectarines, halved and stoned
but unpeeled
2 cups water
1 cup dry rosé wine
1 cup sugar
1 vanilla pod

for serving
blueberries
raspberries
fresh mint

Wash the nectarines and set aside.

Simmer the water, wine, sugar and split vanilla pod in a wide saucepan, stirring until the sugar has dissolved. Add the nectarines to the hot syrup, placing them cut-side down so that they are totally immersed in the syrup. Cook very gently for 5 minutes. Remove from the heat and allow to cool, making sure that they are covered in syrup. If necessary, cover with a plate to keep submerged.

Once cooled, remove with a slotted spoon and reduce the syrup over a high heat until slightly thickened. Pour over the nectarines and refrigerate until well chilled.

Serve with blueberries, raspberries and fresh mint. Do rinse and dry the vanilla and store in a jar of sugar, to use again.

for 4–6

Harvest season
Crates of grapes at Buitenverwachting.

baked whole plums in sweet wine

1 kg greengages or large purple plums
¼ cup soft brown sugar
butter
½ cup sweet hanepoot wine

for serving, mix together
½ cup plain yoghurt
½ cup fresh cream

Rinse and dry the plums. Arrange the whole plums upright in a single layer in a buttered ovenproof dish just large enough to hold them. Sprinkle with the sugar and dot each plum with a bit of butter. Bake at 180 °C for 10 minutes. Pour over the wine and bake for 25 minutes, or until tender, but still holding their shape. Serve warm with the well-chilled yoghurt and cream mix.

for 6

pink champagne jellies

½ cup water
¼ cup castor sugar
1 Tbsp gelatine
2 cups pink champagne or sparkling wine

Heat the water and the sugar, stirring until dissolved. Bring to the boil, then remove from the heat. Sprinkle over the gelatine and stir briskly until dissolved. Strain. Allow to cool for a few minutes, then stir in the champagne. Allow bubbles to settle. Pour into 4–6 champagne flutes. Refrigerate for 2 hours, or until set.

for 4–6

THE GREAT OUTDOORS

It's understandable that the unpredictable climate results in an easy relaxed lifestyle. We don't make definite arrangements. When we plan a barbecue or picnic, we say, 'Let's see what the weather's like.'

the great outdoors

honeyed roast nuts

three-seed brittle

fruit and nut cookies

fresh tuna pâté

roast pumpkin and

parmesan tart

roast chicken with shallots

and rosemary

skewered melon and mint

with lemon-ginger syrup

citrus poppyseed loaf with

berries and crème fraîche

grilled mangoes

barbecued butterflied fish

barbecued spiced

marinated lamb

barbecued vegetables

with three sauces

herbed breads

PAGES 122/123 The Contour Path around Lion's Head.

LEFT Sea Point, from Signal Hill.

trail snacks for mountain walks

Cape Town is situated between mountains and sea. The choice of hikes within minutes of the centre of the city is awesome. My favourite walk to show-off Cape Town to visitors is the easy circular route along the lower slopes of Lion's Head, that spans the city from the harbour to Camps Bay.

honeyed roast nuts

2 Tbsp butter
½ cup honey
100 g brazil nuts
100 g unskinned almonds
100 g walnuts

Use a large microwaveproof bowl so that the syrup doesn't boil over.

First melt the butter, then add the remaining ingredients and mix well together. Microwave on high for 6 minutes, or until it's a deep caramel colour. Turn onto a baking sheet lined with non-stick baking paper. Allow to cool, then break up into pieces. Store in an airtight container.

for 8

three-seed brittle

⅓ cup pumpkin seeds
⅓ cup sunflower seeds
⅓ cup sesame seeds
¼ cup runny honey
¼ cup sugar
2 Tbsp water

Roast the seeds at 180 °C for 5 minutes, or until golden. Boil the honey, sugar and water together until the mixture is a good caramel colour. Add the roasted seeds and stir for 1–2 minutes. Turn onto a sheet of non-stick baking paper and flatten with a spatula. Allow to cool and set, then break into pieces.

for 8

fruit and nut cookies

125 g soft butter
½ cup peanut butter
1 cup brown sugar
1 free-range egg, beaten
¾ cup stone-ground cake flour
½ tsp bicarbonate of soda
a pinch salt
1 cup seedless raisins
100 g pecans or walnuts, chopped
100 g dark chocolate, chopped

Cream the butter, peanut butter and sugar together. Beat in the egg. Add the flour, sifted together with the bicarbonate of soda and salt. Pour boiling water over the raisins and drain. Add to the batter along with the nuts and chocolate. Mix well together. Drop spoonfuls, well-spaced, onto baking sheets lined with non-stick baking paper and bake at 190 °C for 10–12 minutes or until pale golden. Leave to set for 1–2 minutes, then cool on wire racks. If stored in an aitight container, they can be made a few days ahead.

makes about 36

picnic in the forest

On sunny days in winter, or to escape the sun over lunchtime in summer, the forests make perfect picnic places. I love the Glen, it's minutes from where I stay, and one can park pretty close, so it's light work to carry the food, drinks, Sunday papers and the scrabble set.

fresh tuna pâté

400 g filletted tuna in one piece (light meat only)
1 cup dry white wine
1 cup water
1 or 2 slices onion
1 bay leaf
2 or 3 sprigs each celery, parsley and dill
a few peppercorns
¼ cup thick mayonnaise
¼ cup thick cream cheese
strained juice of 1 lemon
5 or 6 slim salad onions, chopped
salt and milled black pepper

Place the tuna in a saucepan small enough to fit snugly. Pour over the wine and water. Add the onion, herbs, peppercorns and a little salt. Bring to a simmer, turn the fish, cover and turn off the heat. Leave to cool in the liquid, by which time the fish should be cooked.

Drain and flake, then pound with the rest of the ingredients. Check seasoning and add more lemon juice if needed.

Serve with radishes and baguette.

for 8

roast pumpkin and parmesan tart

for the pastry

1½ cups stone-ground cake flour

a pinch salt

100 g cold butter

2–3 Tbsp iced water

1 Tbsp olive oil

1 free-range egg, separated

⅓ cup grated parmesan cheese

Sift the flour with the salt. Cut in the butter and rub lightly together with the fingertips until crumbly.

Beat together the iced water, oil and egg yolk. Add to the flour mixture and knead lightly to form a dough. Wrap well and chill for at least 30 minutes. Roll out thinly between 2 sheets of non-stick baking paper, then fit into a 23 cm loose-bottomed tart tin, trimming the edges. Save any leftovers in the freezer. Prick the shell well and freeze while heating the oven to 220 °C. Brush the base with lightly beaten egg white and sprinkle with parmesan cheese. Bake at 220 °C for 10–15 minutes, or until pale golden.

for the filling

500 g peeled pumpkin chunks

salt and milled black pepper

olive oil

sage leaves

3 extra-large free-range eggs

1 cup thick fresh cream

1 clove garlic, crushed

1 Tbsp chopped sage leaves

for the topping

¼ cup grated parmesan cheese

¼ cup fresh breadcrumbs

enough olive oil to moisten lightly

Arrange the pumpkin in a single layer in an oiled roasting pan. Season and moisten with oil. Tuck in sage leaves. Roast at 220 °C for 30 minutes, or until tender. Allow to cool before spooning into the half-baked crust.

Beat the eggs, cream, garlic and chopped sage together, seasoning to taste. Pour over the pumpkin. Mix together the topping ingredients, sprinkle over the filling and bake at 180 °C for 30 minutes, or until set, slightly puffed and golden. Garnish with fresh sage leaves. Good hot, but perfect cooled to room temperature.

for 8

roast chicken
with shallots and rosemary

Nicest at room temperature, so roast on the day of serving.
Serve with baby potatoes dressed with wine vinegar and olive oil, and steamed
green beans tossed with olive oil, lemon juice and shredded basil.

1.5 kg free-range chicken
coarse salt and milled black pepper
2 lemon wedges
2 or 3 bay leaves
2 cloves garlic
sprigs of rosemary
1 Tbsp olive oil
400 g shallots, peeled
¼ cup balsamic vinegar
¼ cup dry red or white wine
¾ cup chicken stock
2 Tbsp runny honey
watercress to garnish

Trim, wash and dry the chicken. Season inside. Thread a short skewer with lemon, bay leaves, garlic and rosemary. Place inside the chicken. Rub skin with coarse salt, black pepper and olive oil. Set aside.

Place the shallots in an oiled roasting pan. Season and pour over the vinegar, wine and stock. Add sprigs of rosemary and cover with a sheet of oiled greaseproof paper. Bake at 190 °C for 30 minutes. Remove from the oven, discard the paper and increase the heat to 230 °C. Place the chicken, breast-side up, in the middle of the roasting pan, pushing the shallots aside. Roast at 230 °C for 1 hour, or until nicely browned and the shallots are very tender.

Mix the honey with a little of the pan juices and spoon over the chicken and shallots. Roast for another 10–15 minutes, or until well glazed. Turn off the oven and, leaving the door ajar, allow to cool to room temperature. Garnish with lots of watercress.

for 6–8

skewered melon
and mint with lemon-ginger syrup

1 sweet melon or papino
fresh mint leaves
berries
¼ cup honey
1 Tbsp crushed fresh ginger
juice of 2 lemons

Cut the melon into wedges. Peel and discard the seeds. Cut into chunks and thread onto skewers with mint leaves and berries of your choice. Simmer the honey, ginger and strained lemon juice together for a few minutes. Allow to cool completely, then spoon over the fruit. Chill until serving.

for 6

watermelon and feta salad

I love this salad, the contrast of the sweet melon and the salty cheese. Serve it ice-cold. It is said to originate in Israel, but features in the cookbooks of the best contemporary chefs. Alternate chunks of melon with feta and basil leaves, drizzle with olive oil and strew with a few toasted pumpkin seeds. Add a grinding of black pepper. It's a perfect cheese course to match the informality of a summer picnic or barbecue.

citrus poppyseed loaf
with berries and crème fraîche

⅓ cup poppy seeds
¾ cup full-cream milk
zest of 1 large bright lemon
zest of 1 bright orange
180 g unsalted butter, at
room temperature
1 cup castor sugar
3 extra-large free-range eggs
2 cups cake flour
2½ tsp baking powder
a pinch salt

for the syrup
½ cup strained orange juice
¾ cup strained lemon juice
½ cup sugar
1 small lemon, thinly sliced and halved

for serving
fresh berries
crème fraîche

Soak the poppy seeds in milk for 45 minutes.

Pour boiling water over the thin strips of lemon and orange zest, then drain.

Cream the butter and sugar until pale and fluffy. Beat in the eggs, one at a time. Sift the flour, baking powder and salt together, and fold into the beaten mixture, alternating with the milk and seeds. Lastly fold in the zest.

Turn into a buttered loaf pan lined with non-stick baking paper. Bake at 180 °C for 45 minutes or until a tester comes out clean. Allow to cool for about 5 minutes before turning out. Invert the loaf over a plate and prick all over.

Simmer the syrup ingredients together for 5 minutes. Slowly spoon the warm syrup over the warm cake. Serve at room temperature with berries and crème fraîche.

for 10

barbecue on the beach

South Africans love to braai – that's the local name, Afrikaans, for barbecue. As in America, it originates from the early pioneers. The Dutch farmers 'trekked' across the country in ox wagons to get away from their British rulers. So what started from practical considerations, is now a popular way of entertaining – anything from a B.Y.O.B. on the beach to a rather glamorous affair on the terrace at home.

grilled mangoes

4 firm ripe mangoes, peeled

for the dressing
1 Tbsp balsamic vinegar
1 Tbsp fresh lemon juice
⅓ cup sunflower oil
salt and milled black pepper to taste

Cut off the cheeks of the mangoes as close to the pip as possible. Arrange on an oiled grid. Grill over hot coals until starting to catch. Turn onto a platter.

Mix the dressing ingredients together and pour over the mangoes. Good with grilled fish or chicken.

for 4

Swimming pool at Maiden's Cove, Clifton
Barbecue with a view of Camps Bay and the Apostles. Or choose to barbecue at Oudekraal.

barbecued butterflied fish

Choose whatever's freshest that day. Use fresh snoek when in season, as it's best on the barbecue. My fishmonger insists that only snoek from cold currents is good. Make up a jar of dressing and use some to moisten the fish as it comes off the coals. But it's also good on hot potatoes, steamed or baked, on steamed greens, or with a chunky mixed salad.

1 whole fish (1.5–2 kg), cleaned and butterflied
olive oil
Atlantic sea salt and milled black pepper

for the dressing
¼ cup wine vinegar
2 cloves garlic, crushed
2 tsp mustard, Dijon or powder
1 cup good olive oil
salt and milled black pepper to taste
a handful chopped fresh herbs (basil, Italian parsley, dill, oregano, coriander or a mix)

First make the dressing by mixing all the ingredients together.

Rinse the fish. Dry well. Make a few slashes in the flesh. Oil and season. Place the fish on a well-oiled grid. You could even spray it with a non-stick cooking spray. Barbecue over hot coals until the skin crisps and the flesh is just cooked and still moist. Remove to a large platter and immediately pour over the dressing.

for 6–8

barbecued spiced marinated lamb

Works beautifully in a Weber over medium-hot coals, covered and cooked for
45 minutes, turning now and again, or until well browned but pink inside.

1.5 kg butterflied leg of lamb

for the marinade
2 cups thin plain yoghurt
2 cloves garlic, crushed
1 tsp dried origanum
1 tsp dried mint
1 tsp ground cumin
1 tsp coarsely ground coriander seeds (use a
disposable spice mill)
salt and milled black pepper to taste

for the sauce
2-3 tsp cornflour mixed with water
until smooth

for serving
warm pita breads
olive oil sprinkled with dukkah (from good
food shops)

on the side
baby spinach leaves, washed and dried

Mix together the marinade ingredients
and marinate the lamb overnight in the
refrigerator. Allow to come to room
temperature while preparing the fire. Remove
from the marinade and pat dry. Cook as
instructed above.

Whisk the leftover marinade with the cornflour
paste and heat, stirring, until slightly thickened.

Serve warm with the sliced lamb, along with
wedges of pita stuffed with spinach leaves
and dipped into the spiced olive oil. (First
warm the pitas on the braai.) Steamed
basmati rice mixed with spinach, lemon
juice and chopped dill, would also make
a good side dish, served warm, or at
room temperature.

for 6

barbecued vegetables with three sauces

Use a Weber to barbecue a selection of vegetables. Brush with olive oil, but season with salt and milled black pepper only after they are cooked. Use whatever's available and looks good. Quartered butternut squash or wedges of pumpkin, corn on the cob, large open mushrooms, halved sweet peppers, whole baby marrows. See that the coals are not too fierce, and cook covered. Remove the vegetables as they are ready.

to make garlic-herb butter
Pound 125 g softened unsalted butter, at room temperature, with 2–3 crushed cloves garlic, 2–3 Tbsp chopped parsley and 2–3 Tbsp snipped chives. A lemon rind, shredded and blanched, may be added. Add salt and milled black pepper to taste. Wrap in greaseproof paper and refrigerate.

to make Italian anchovy cream sauce
Reduce, until slightly thickened, 1 cup fresh cream with 4 or 5 chopped anchovies, 1 crushed clove garlic and a grinding of black pepper. Serve hot or at room temperature.

to make Thai green curry sauce
Stir-fry 1–2 Tbsp Thai green curry paste, then mix in a can of coconut milk, 1 chopped fresh green chilli (optional), 1 crushed clove garlic, and the chopped tender centre of a stalk or two of lemon grass. Leave to reduce and thicken slightly. Add Thai fish sauce to taste, and some chopped coriander and basil leaves. Serve hot or at room temperature.

s u n s e t   s a n d w i c h e s

There are stunning sunsets in Cape Town, as the sun sets over the sea. My favourite neighbourhood spot is Bakoven. It is breathtakingly beautiful to sit on the rocks and take in the background of mountains and the crashing waves below. It's bliss to take a picnic basket of chilled white wine and good sandwiches to share with friends. Of course, you can buy bread for the sandwiches. Panini or pumpkin seed rolls. Chunks of crusty baguettes, or thickly sliced sourdough bread. All are good. But I happen to love baking bread. And if I'm free on a Sunday, relaxing at home, I enjoy the task in anticipation of the picnic in the evening.

herbed breads

3 cups bread flour
1½ tsp instant dried yeast
a pinch salt
olive oil
1 cup warm water
fresh herbs (sage leaves, sprigs of thyme and rosemary)
salt and milled black pepper

Mix the flour with the yeast and salt. Stir in 2 Tbsp olive oil and enough water to make a soft dough. Knead well on a floured board for 5–10 minutes or until smooth and elastic. Place the ball of dough in an oiled bowl, turn around to grease all over, cover and leave for 30 minutes, or until risen. Punch down and knead lightly.

Divide into 12 pieces and shape with your hands into small, flat rounds. Place on an oiled baking sheet. Press in a mix of fresh herbs. Brush with olive oil and grind over salt and pepper. Allow to stand for 5–10 minutes, then bake at 230 °C for 15 minutes, or until golden.

makes 12

suggested fillings
smoked chicken, green asparagus,
    mayonnaise and watercress
proscuitto, drunken pecorino and rocket
roasted vegetables, hummus and cos lettuce

GOOD FOOD SHOPS

Atlas Trading Store Co.
94 Wale St, City. Tel. 423-4361

Carluccis
22 Upper Orange St, Oranjezicht.
Tel. 465-0795
29 Victoria Rd, Bantry Bay.
Tel. 439-6476

Fields Health Store
84 Kloof St, Tamboerskloof.
Tel. 423-9587

Food International Shop
7 Abfred Court, St Johns Rd, Sea Point.
Tel. 434-0760

Giovanni's Deliworld
103 Main Rd, Green Point.
Tel. 434-6893

Melissas Food Shop
94 Kloof St, Tamboerskloof.
Tel. 424-5540
3 Cardiff Castle Centre,
cnr Kildare Rd & Main St, Newlands.
Tel. 683-6949
Shop 1 & 2, Constantia Courtyard,
Constantia. Tel. 794-4696

Morgenster shop, Morgenster Estate
Somerset West (take Vergelegen
turnoff at Lourensford Rd).
Tel. 852-1738

Muldersvlei Market (Klein Joostenberg)
Muldersvlei (off the R 304).
Tel. 884-4208

New York Bagels
51 Regent Rd, Sea Point.
Tel. 439-7523

Ondersteun Handelaars
52–54 Salt River Market, Salt River.
Tel. 448-1491

Pasta Freddi
Shop 35, Constantia Village, Constantia.
Tel. 794-3694

TOP TABLEWARE

Africa Nova
Shop C3, 72 Waterkant St,
Cape Quarter, Green Point.
Tel. 425-5123

@ Home
Cavendish Sq, Claremont. Tel. 670-3984
Canal Walk, Century City. Tel. 529-3152

Bright House
97 Bree St, City. Tel. 424-9024
Cavendish Sq, Claremont. Tel. 683-6012

Delagoa
Shop 002, Clock Tower Centre,
V & A Waterfront. Tel. 425-3787

Heartworks
98 Kloof St, Gardens. Tel. 424-8419
Shop 51b, Gardens Centre, Gardens.
Tel. 465-3289

House and Interiors at Bric-a-Brac Lane
1 Corwen St, Claremont. Tel. 683-1468

LIM
86a Kloof St, Gardens. Tel. 423-1200

Loft Living
122 Kloof St, Gardens. Tel. 422-1517

Nocturnal Affair
16 Cavendish St, Claremont.
Tel. 683-8186
Gardens Centre, Gardens. Tel. 461-7412
V&A Wharf, Waterfront. Tel. 419-2291

The Yellow Door
Gardens Centre, Gardens. Tel. 465-4702

BEST BITES

Take home, take-out or eat in
Antipasto. Part of a country-style
Italian lunch. La Masseria,
cnr Bluegum & Huguenot St,
Evertsdal, Durbanville.
Tel. 880-0266

Berry tarts. Hillcrest berry farm (off R 310),
Stellenbosch. Tel. 885-1629

Grilled calamari and roast potato wedges.
Harbour House, Kalk Bay Harbour.
Tel. 788-4133

Mussels Belgian-style. Den Anker,
Pierhead, V&A Waterfront.
Tel. 419-0249

Nice ice cream. Contact The Nice
Company for details of stockists.
Tel. 715-3379

Pancakes. Savoury traditional bobotie
or sweet green fig preserve. Harrie's
Pancakes, Clock Tower Centre,
V&A Waterfront. Tel. 421-0887

Rotis. Zorina's Cafe, 172 Loop St, City.
Tel. 424-9301

Smoked salmon. French Smokery,
La Maison du Fumée, 78 Main Rd,
Sea Point. Tel. 434-7950

Smoked snoek. Palace Fish Shop,
533 Albert Rd, Salt River.
Tel. 447-0450

Spinach and feta pies. The Pumpkin Shop,
12 Kloof Nek Rd, Tamboerskloof.
Tel. 423-6553

Tea and scones. The courtyard at
Winchester Mansions Hotel,
221 Beach Rd, Sea Point.
Tel. 434-2351

Thin-crust pizza. Limoncello, 8 Breda St,
Gardens. Tel. 461-5100

Trotters with porcini-cream sauce.
Marios, 89 Main Rd, Green Point.
Tel. 439-6644

ON THE WINE SIDE

Bread and wine. Môreson Wine Farm,
Happy Valley Rd, Franschhoek.
Casual lunches. Tel. 876-3692

Buitenverwachting. Klein Constantia Rd,
Constantia. Fine dining, casual courtyard lunches and picnics. Tel. 794-3522

T A K E   N O T E

Raith Gourmet
38 Gardens Centre, Mill St, Gardens.
Tel. 465-2729

Spar
Regent Rd, Sea Point. Tel. 439-0913

Taste of Japan
41–43 Paarden Eiland Rd,
Paarden Eiland. Tel. 706-7690

Woolworths Foods
Stores throughout the Western Cape.
Tel. 407-9111

Ciabatta bread. Olympia Cafe and Deli,
134 Main Rd, Kalk Bay. Tel. 788-6396

Eggs Benedict. Spaanschemat River Café,
Constantia Uitsig Farm, Spaanschemat
River Rd, Constantia. Tel. 794-3010

Fried calamari and chips. Fish on the
Rocks. Harbour Rd, Hout Bay Harbour.
Tel. 790-1153

Fried fish and chips. Garden's Fisheries,
3 Vredehoek Ave, Vredehoek.
Tel. 465-3512

Constantia Uitsig. Good food with a
great view. Tel. 794-4480

Lady Phillips Restaurant. At Vergelegen,
Lourensford Rd, Somerset West. Lunches
plus picnics in season. Tel. 847-1346

Tokara. Helshoogte Pass, Stellenbosch.
Sophisticated eating. Tel. 808-5959

PLEASE NOTE: All Cape Town and environs
telephone numbers are preceded by an
(021) code.